OUR STORIES, OUR LIVES

In the Mirror of Your Heart

The Personal Journeys of Four Women

Edited by Donna Streufert

LWML

Scripture quotations marked NIV are taken from THE HOLY BIBLE, NEW INTERNATIONAL VERSION®. Copyright © 1973, 1978, 1984 by the International Bible Society. Used by permission of Zondervan Publishing House. All rights reserved.

The "NIV" and "New International Version" trademarks are registered in the United States Patent and Trademark Office by the International Bible Society. Use of either trademark requires the permission of the International Bible Society.

Copyright © 1995 The International Lutheran Women's Missionary League
3558 S. Jefferson Avenue, St. Louis, MO 63118-3910

Printed by Concordia Publishing House
3558 S. Jefferson Avenue, St. Louis, MO 63118-3968
Manufactured in the United States of America

All rights reserved. No part of this publication may be reproduced, stored in a retrieval system, or transmitted, in any form or by any means, electronic, mechanical, photocopying, recording, or otherwise, without the prior written permission of The International Lutheran Women's Missionary League.

Contents

Preface   5

Acknowledgments   9

Story 1
    Rebecca: Broken Wings, Mended Hearts   13
    An Encouraging Word   39
    Reflection   49

Story 2
    Kim: All Things New   53
    An Encouraging Word   73
    Reflection   82

Story 3
    Connie: A Path Unplanned   87
    An Encouraging Word   110
    Guidelines for Handling Value Conflicts   119
    Reflection   121

Story 4
    Ruth: Time Enough   125
    An Encouraging Word   151
    Reflection   159

Preface

About this series ...

Sharing experiences is an important part of a woman's life. Talking, listening, laughing, and crying together; exchanging ideas, advice, and counsel; being close by; being companions and sisters and mentors to one another—all are part of the experience we women share.

Women offer encouragement to one another as we share our personal struggles, our dark valleys, and our bright horizons. Women share love with a listening ear, a warm embrace, the assurance of forgiveness, or a word of counsel. Women understand when the author of Hebrews writes, "Encourage one another daily, as long as it is called Today" (Heb. 3:13 NIV).

This book is the second in the series Our Stories, Our Lives. Similar to the first book, *A Place to Rest Your Heart*, it offers words of encouragement written by women, for women. In this volume, four women relate their personal journeys. Their stories reflect the true-life experiences of women in different places and in different stages of life.

Each woman's story is followed by insights and analysis written by a professional Christian counselor. She uses her expertise to help the reader recognize what is going on in the character's emotional and spiritual life and offers Christian guidance and encouragement.

Next is a section designed for personal reflection. Here is an opportunity to grow in understanding, to sort out your own thoughts about the challenges portrayed in the story, and to draw support from God's Word to face these challenges.

We hope all this will encourage you to share your own experiences with other women.

After you read the four stories in this book, give it to a friend, a sister, a fellow traveler in the faith. Ask about her feelings. Compare reactions to the stories. Use it as a means for personal growth and Christian witness. Encourage. Share. Counsel. Hug. Rejoice—together—woman to woman!

Men, too, may gain insight into women's experiences, needs, feelings, and reactions through this series!

About the personal journeys of four women ...

In the opening story, "Broken Wings, Mended Hearts," author Louise Mueller profiles Rebecca. Readers follow Becky as she moves through shock, grief, despair, and anger during the first six months of divorce. Becky's journal, which her support-group leader suggests she keep, reflects her feelings and experiences living through divorce. Readers also glimpse the pain and experiences of other men and women in Becky's support group. Becky, supported not only by members of her group but also by the wise counsel of her pastor, learns the deeper meaning of repentance and forgiveness. She learns to live with what the Lord has given [her] and to wait patiently for His next step. She learns that there is "life after divorce."

In "All Things New," author Lauren Beale tells the story of Kim, a first-time mother holding a new life in her arms. Everything has changed for Kim—physically, emotionally, relationally. Life will never be quite the same. Kim admits that no "childbirth class or conversation with other new parents could ever have prepared us for this odd, confusing, frustrating, tear-filled yet miraculous" time! Kim and husband Bruce "rely on God's promises and cherish the prayers of His people" as they experience long hours of labor, the joy of holding their baby, the mysteries of apnea, the pain of temporary separation, and the possibility of serious health problems. But through all this, plus the *normal* challenges of meeting baby needs and adjusting to a new life-style as a family of three, Kim's reliance on God's strength, her faith in His goodness, and her desire to be an instrument of His peace in the lives of her husband and child inspire all women who have traveled that life-changing journey to motherhood.

In "A Path Unplanned," author Kathleen Winkler tells Connie's story. Connie, too, is a mother full of hopes and dreams for her children, yet Connie's dream of "a wonderful Christian home with wonderful Christian children" did not come true exactly as she expected. Although Connie and Carl committed their lives to the Lord, went to church, and tried to raise their children to be fine, upstanding Christians, both their son and their daughter rebelled in their teens and adopted life-styles that crushed their parents, alienated family members, and tore them apart. Still, this is a story of the triumph of a family's love over huge odds, over enormous conflict. Carl and Connie struggle to face their son's homosexuality and their daughter's live-in relationship with her boyfriend. "I wanted to have a nervous breakdown. I wanted to just go away and pull the covers over my head and wake up when it was all gone, but I couldn't do that. ... I had this horrible thing always in the back of my mind." With the help of counselors and Christian friends, Connie at last learns to understand that her job is to love her children, and God's job is to change them.

In "Time Enough," author Annette Frank introduces readers to Ruth, a not-too-typical working mother. As Ruth reminisces on a beautiful, peaceful Saturday morning, she admits that often life has seemed out of control, as though she were in a "race car barrelling down a track, hardly able to glimpse a passing flag." She remembers times when resources were limited and serious decisions had to be made. She remembers how life has changed as her children have grown older. She remembers when time and money have been tight and stretched thin. She remembers learning to approach problems creatively and cooperatively. Through it all Ruth relies on God: "He loves me. When everything else seems upset and too much to cope with, I have His love. I see it best through Phil, Rachel, and Josh. Phil said home should be an oasis, a place to come for refreshment and quiet. I think God has given us that. But I think it's because He dwells in our house." In Him, Ruth finds time for everything.

As you share the personal journeys of these women, you may find yourself in their shoes. Or you may feel yourself growing in empathy and understanding for women who face challenges you have not yet faced. Or you may know women like those profiled here. You may have a friend who could benefit from knowing she is not alone in her *own* struggle—just as you and I are also *not* alone.

Donna Streufert, Editor

Acknowledgments

In this inspirational book, you are going to meet four women whose personal journeys will touch your life. The authors of these stories are also engaged in their own unique faith journeys. Take a moment to meet them.

Louise Mueller, author of "Rebecca," edited the *Lutheran Woman's Quarterly* for six years, has contributed articles to *The Lutheran Witness* and *Portals of Prayer*. She served on The Lutheran Church—Missouri Synod's task force to study the role of women in the church and on the LCMS Commission on Women. Currently, Louise is collecting the stories of the women who served in the foreign missions of the church, particularly in India. The book will be published by the LWML as its contribution to the 100th anniversary of the beginning of the Synod's foreign missions.

Lauren Beale, author of "Kim," graduated from Valparaiso University with a major in journalism. Today she is a freelance writer specializing in public relations and employee communications. In 1983, Lauren won a Gold Quill Award of Excellence from the International Association of Business Communicators (IABC). She has served on the staff of the *Lutheran Woman's Quarterly* and has published devotional material for women. Named an Outstanding Young Woman of America in 1987, Lauren is wife of Marshall and mother of Joshua and Andrea.

Kathleen Winkler, author of "Connie," has written medical education publications for several hospitals. She writes regularly on medical topics, education, and social issues for local and regional magazines. The author of *When the Crying Stops: Abortion, the Pain and the Healing* (Northwestern, 1992), Kathleen is presently working on a parent education book for CPH.

Annette Frank, author of "Ruth," is employed full time outside of her home. She is the wife of a Lutheran teacher and church musician and mother of two teenagers who are active in their church, school, and part-time jobs. Annette serves on several carefully chosen programs at her children's high school, teaches Sunday school, and is a student (recently she earned a paralegal certificate, passing her orals with distinction). She has authored junior high Sunday school curriculum and articles for *The Lutheran Witness* and *Teachers Interaction*.

Shirley Schaper is a family and marriage counselor. Shirley wrote the counselor sections for "Rebecca," "Kim," and "Ruth." She also contributed to the first book in this series, *A Place to Rest Your Heart*. Shirley and her husband have one daughter.

Dr. Beverly Yahnke, a licensed psychologist, is the founder and director of a Christian counseling clinic in Milwaukee, Wisconsin. She wrote the counselor section for "Connie." Bev is a frequent speaker for educator conferences as well as school and church groups. She is a sincere advocate for children, promoting family values and excellence in Christian education.

Donna Streufert, general editor, is a teacher and writer who resides in South Bend, Indiana. Donna serves on the editorial staff of the *Lutheran Woman's Quarterly*. She writes regularly for a devotional guide for families with children and develops religion curriculum materials for children and adults.

Story 1

Rebecca: Broken Wings, Mended Hearts

by Louise Mueller

Rebecca

September 7, 1989

How did I get myself into this journal writing anyway? Do I really want to record this terrible time in my life?

It was Judy who decided I need a divorce support group—and Judy is very persistent. Not only is she well-organized but, as Jack used to say, "If you let her, she'll run your life too."

That's not a nice thing to say. Judy and Dave have been true friends through all of this mess. Nonetheless, when Judy gets an idea, she runs with it. Not only did she suggest a support group, she called Pastor Keller to locate one, and he recommended this nondenominational Christian group.

"After all," said Judy, "it's better than sitting in that big house by yourself and moping." She's right, of course. It's been more than two months since Jack left, and I know I need to get on with my life.

So tonight I went.

Marcia, our group leader, suggested that we keep a journal. She says it will help us work through our feelings. She labels divorce "a grief experience."

Grief? Yes, but that wasn't my initial response. After the first shock, it was despair—total, complete despair. I'd crawl into bed and curl myself up into a little ball and try to feel God's presence all around me, shutting out the terrible darkness, the feeling that I was utterly alone. I'd try to pray, but all I could think of was that Bible passage that says when you don't know how to pray, just groan.

It couldn't have happened at a worse time! My father had

died a few months earlier, and in late June, I spent a week in Nebraska helping my mother pack and move into a small apartment. Jack met my plane when I came back to California. He seemed distant and preoccupied, but I, too, was absorbed in the grief of closing my childhood home with all its memories and didn't feel much like talking either. As we pulled into the driveway, Jack suddenly announced, "Becky, while you were gone, I moved out."

I stared at him in disbelief, my mouth open.

"But Jack," I blurted. "Why?"

"Come on, Becky! You know things haven't been good between us these past couple years."

"But we can work things out! I know we can! I suggested that we see a marriage counselor. Let's talk to Pastor Keller—won't you at least try *that?*"

"It's too late, Becky. Face it! It's over!"

Suddenly, I asked the hidden question. "Is there someone else?"

"Don't be so naive, Becky. Don't tell me you didn't know!"

I guess I should have. There were those evenings Jack stayed at the office so late, the weekend business trips, his unresponsiveness to affection, the infrequency of our sex life. But I didn't want to admit that my marriage was falling apart, and so I denied the evidence.

Everyone else knew. Even the children.

Jack carried my bags into the bedroom, gave me a quick peck on the cheek, and then I heard his car drive away. I walked to the closet and saw his side completely cleaned out. So was his chest of drawers. And the medicine cabinet. I stood there in the middle of that emptiness, and the phone rang. It was Jane.

"Mother," she said, "welcome home! How was your trip?"

"Oh, Jane, your father just moved out!"

"So he finally decided he wanted that slut!" she exclaimed. "I'll be right over!"

And when John called from the university several days later and I repeated what had happened, he asked, "Did he move in with his girlfriend?"

The children have been very supportive. After all, I've been a good, protective mother, giving them care and love, always there when Jack was involved with his business (and *other* things). Jane even offered to move back home for a while, but her apartment is close to her job. Besides, she and Zach will be getting married next month; she shouldn't have to take on my troubles.

September 14

All this week I told myself I wouldn't go back to the support group. But I knew that if I didn't, I'd face Judy's reproaches and, coward that I am, I went.

It's a small group. So far there are five of us. Elsie is in her 50s. She wears high heels and rather tight slacks, lots of jewelry, and her blonde hair (obviously from a bottle) is carefully styled.

Shirley is a shy, rather bedraggled and forlorn young woman who seems to cringe when attention turns to her.

Emily is quite young. She wears sneakers and sweats and has her long brown hair in a ponytail. There's a harried, preoccupied look about her and little tension lines around her eyes.

Marcia, our leader, is a trained psychologist; she has been divorced for about four years.

And then there's me, Rebecca Carlson, age 42, with my smiling face painted on, sitting apart, resistant to sharing my problems with a group of comparative strangers.

We all sat there; no one seemed to want to start a conversation. So Marcia said, "Well, in getting acquainted with one another last week, we found we all have two things in common. We're Christian women, and we're going through a divorce. How do those two things go together?"

They don't.

Elsie summed it up for us. "I was raised in a strict, German family. My father-in-law was a Lutheran minister. I've always believed that marriage is 'till death us do part.' I can't believe this is happening to me!"

"Then it was a surprise?" goaded Marcia.

We nodded.

"You had no warning that there was trouble in your marriage?" Marcia persisted.

Well, that was a little different.

"I thought all couples had their bad times," said Emily.

"I guess I just pretended it wasn't there," said Elsie, thoughtfully.

So we talked about denial.

That's where I am, I think. This is a bad dream, and one day I'll wake up and find it isn't so. For quite a while I didn't even tell anyone that I was alone—the people at work, the couples Jack and I socialized with, my Bible study group, not even Pastor Keller. I just couldn't bring myself to say, "My husband has left me," because if I didn't say it, I could pretend it hadn't happened.

Every morning when I got up, I'd feel I was pulling a mask over my head. I'd put on my clothes, paint on my smile, and say, "I'm just fine," while inside I was completely devastated. Then I'd come home and sit in front of the TV watching anything that would absorb my attention and knitting furiously. In two months I've finished three sweaters!

I hid the real me so well I couldn't even cry—I still can't.

About two weeks after Jack left, he called and asked if he could pick up some tools from the garage.

"Hello, Beck," he said quietly as I let him in the door.

"Hello, Jack," I said dully.

"Becky," he said, "I'm sorry I shocked you so. I realize it was a double whammy to move out so soon after your dad's death. But I had to do it then; if I'd waited until you were back home I would never have had the nerve."

"But why, Jack?" I asked again. "Haven't I been a good wife?"

"You have been a very good wife, Becky. Fact is, you're too good for me."

"Then how could you get involved with someone else?" I persisted.

"Mandy needs me."

"I need you too!" I wailed.

"No, you don't," he said. "Becky, you are a very strong woman. You will survive without me. I'm the only one Mandy has. Besides, she makes me feel young."

"But we're not young. We're middle-aged. What's wrong with that?"

"Becky, I want a divorce," he said, not looking me in the eye. "It's the only way. You can keep the house, and I'll give you a generous settlement."

"A divorce! Jack, Christians don't divorce!"

"Then I guess I'm not as good a Christian as you are either!" he said sharply. "I think it would be better if you initiated the divorce. Bob Johnson is a good lawyer, and you know him pretty well. Why not let him handle it?"

I sat there not answering. After a few moments of silence, Jack said quietly, "Good-bye, Becky."

I didn't initiate the divorce, and I didn't talk to Bob Johnson. Twenty years of marriage can't end this way! If I bide my time, Jack will come to his senses. One day he'll be walking in that door and he'll say, "Becky, I'm sorry. Will you forgive me?" I'm a good Christian; I'll be able to put this behind me, and we'll start over again. That's what I keep telling myself will happen.

It hasn't.

September 20

It had to happen one day! This afternoon I came face-to-face with Jack's new love. I was hurrying into the mall to pick up the dress I'd ordered for Jane's wedding, and I almost ran into them.

"Hello, Becky," said Jack, a little embarrassed. "This is Mandy."

We stared at each other. She is blonde, baby-faced, somewhat plump—and very young. She held on to Jack's arm possessively, moving closer, and looking up at him adoringly. And she is obviously pregnant!

Back home I was suddenly very angry. The nerve of that

man! How dare he walk out on me? And for such a simpering, clinging vine—the very type of woman he used to make fun of! I saw my dirty coffee cup on the kitchen counter and realized it was one of a set Jack and I had purchased at a pottery factory on one of our vacations. I impulsively hurled it to the floor. Then I went to the cupboard and took the rest of the matching mugs and deliberately broke them, too, one by one.

September 22

I'm still seething!

John is home for the weekend, and he and Jack played golf this morning; they have a good father-son relationship, and I'm glad that it continues. Usually I manage to be in another part of the house when they go off together, but this morning I was waiting as Jack came whistling up the walk. As soon as I opened the door, I let him have it with both barrels.

"How could you do this to me?" I screamed. "I've had the rug pulled out from under me, my whole life changed, and nobody asked me if I wanted it that way! Where do my feelings come in anyway? You're doing what you want to do, and no one cares how I feel!"

It was quite a head of steam I had built up, and when it was vented I felt exhausted and quite ashamed. "I'm sorry," I mumbled to John who had walked in and was standing to one side. I was surprised to see a spark of admiration in his eyes.

"That's my old mom again!" he said. "I'm glad to see you've gotten back your spunk!"

Jack remained quiet as they walked out together.

September 25

Today I had another jolt back into the world of reality. In the mail was the summons; Jack has filed for divorce. Knowing that he needs to legitimize his mistress' baby explains why he's been in such a hurry. It doesn't help my anger, my feeling of being used.

September 28

At our support group tonight, we talked about anger, and I tried to analyze why it so suddenly erupted and what I am really angry about. I stand here, wronged and wounded, and there isn't a thing I can do about it. The most important decision for the direction my future will take is being made, and I have no voice in it. For the first time in my life, I'm out of control.

Marcia asked if I am angry with God. I don't think so. God didn't do this to me—Jack did!

However, I can empathize with Emily's reaction. "Why did this happen to me?" she asked. "I'm a good person. I've been a good wife. I'm a good mother."

Emily's Story

I met Carl while I was in high school. In his junior year, he dropped out and went to trade school—he's a carpenter. In spite of my parents' reservations, we got married as soon as I graduated. Carl is an only child; his parents are divorced. He'd tell me how wonderful it was to be part of a large, loving family like mine.

We had more than our share of fights; we're both pretty stubborn. But we'd make up again, and it was wonderful. Carl makes good money—when he works. But four children in three years puts a drain on the budget. (Twins run in my family.) Carl isn't too good with money; he buys big, expensive things—perhaps because he never had them as a child. So we have this huge house with a big mortgage and his clunker of a station wagon, and when Carl was laid off for a while, it was pretty hard to make the payments. I taught an aerobics class evenings to help out.

Carl's last layoff lasted six months, and things really got tight. One of our friends got me a job in his accounting firm while Carl stayed home with the kids. He sat in front of the television and drank beer, and I'd come home and find the baby with soaked, dirty diapers and peanut butter and jelly spread out on the kitchen counter. I guess I did my share of nagging.

When Carl went back to work, he bought himself a motorcycle. Then he told me he's tired of supporting a family—but he didn't move out. I came home from work on one of his days off and found the children alone. The baby was yelling and Jenny was trying to comfort him—she's not quite four years old—and the twins were writing on the wall with a ballpoint pen. I got so mad, I kicked Carl out! Now he's living with his mom, but he still comes over. He says he wants to see his children.

So now I'm stuck with his kids and all his debts while he goes merrily on his way! Why did God let this happen to me? I don't deserve it!

"What do you think you deserve, Emily?" asked Marcia.

"I guess I really don't *deserve* anything from God," she said thoughtfully. "The good times of my marriage were a gift from Him."

But why did this happen to *me?* Emily and Carl were obviously too young and immature to face the responsibilities of marriage and a house full of babies. That certainly wasn't our experience. Jack and I met while I was in nursing school and he was at the university. We were both in our early 20s when we married. Jack was still in college, and I was able to manage for both of us on my nurse's salary.

Those skimping days are long behind us. Jack is a broker and has his own firm. We have a beautiful home and two wonderful children and have been active in our church—me more than Jack. But I realized he hasn't always lived as a Christian, and his work took most of his energy. As time went on, the work and amassing the money seemed to be more and more important to him, while I became more and more involved in church activities and in the part-time nursing position I'd taken to fill my empty-nest blues. Is that what pulled us apart?

October 4

"My husband walked out on me, so why do I feel guilty?" That's what I asked Pastor Keller today. He's been such a supportive spiritual counselor, listening quietly when I vent my despair and anger, never condemning or preaching.

That's why I was so surprised at his answer. "Becky, you are guilty." I stared at him. "Divorce is the final ending of a marriage that has already gone sour," he explained patiently. "The breakup of a relationship is almost never the fault of one partner. Even if it's 99 percent Jack's fault and 1 percent yours, you have failed that 1 percent. You are human; you can't be perfect.

"But," he continued, "our loving Lord forgives our human failings and weaknesses. Whenever those feelings of guilt come, you can say, 'Jesus loves me, and He has forgiven me. The past is behind me.' "

That's easier said than done.

October 6

"What did I do wrong?" That question keeps coming up at our group meetings. Last night Marcia said, "Let's talk some more about why this happened to you. Do you feel that it's your fault?"

Suddenly, quiet little Shirley spoke up: "It's all my fault."

Shirley's Story

> It was always my fault. When Bud would knock me around, he'd tell me it was my fault. I'd done something wrong, and that made him mad. But I never knew what triggered him. I'd try hard to be good, and first thing I knew, there he was yelling and swinging at me.
>
> Once, when I was visiting my mother-in-law, she saw the big bruises on my arm, and I told her Bud had hit me. She said, "Oh, Shirley, Bud is such a good man. You must have done something awful bad to make him that angry." And when I tried to talk to my mother, she wouldn't listen. I think she was afraid I might move

home again, and she's got all she can handle with Pop's drinking and the younger children around.

Mama is always spouting Scripture; she knows the Bible forwards and backwards. She goes to church every Sunday and to prayer meetings on Wednesday. She's so religious, sometimes I think that's what drives Pop to drink. "A woman's life isn't easy; that's the curse God put on us," she said to me. " 'Wives, be subject to your husbands' it says in the Good Book. You be a good wife, Shirley, and maybe Bud will stop hitting you."

But he didn't. I thought maybe after the baby came things would be different. Then one night, Bud got so mad he pushed me down the stairs. It knocked me out and scared him, so he took me to the hospital—of course he said it was an accident. But that night, I miscarried.

We all stared at Shirley in horror. So that's why she is such a frightened little mouse!

"But that's abuse!" I cried. "You don't have to take that. No one does!"

"The first time anyone laid a hand on me, I'd walk out," said Emily.

Elsie didn't say anything. She just walked over and put her arms around Shirley as she wept.

"Shirley came to the abuse center where I work," said Marcia quietly. "We're trying to help her put her life back together."

"I just couldn't go back with Bud again," cried Shirley. "I just couldn't! He made me lose my baby, and I wanted that baby so bad!"

None of us felt like talking as we left the meeting.

Of course I am aware of spouse abuse. But this is the first time I've really known a victim. At least I didn't have to deal with that! Jack may be a tough businessman, but underneath he is a very kind, sensitive man. I don't think he ever consciously

22

hurt anyone.

But I'm hurting! It hurts to talk to Bob Johnson about dividing all the things Jack and I amassed together. It hurts to face Jane's wedding and know that Jack will be there, but we're not a couple anymore. I feel like a worn-out toy that's been discarded!

October 15

Jane and Zach were married last evening. The wedding has been a mixed blessing. All of the preparations have taken my mind off my problems and helped me snap out of my depression. At the same time, her glow of happiness makes me cringe—I keep praying it will last.

Jack's role in the ceremony was a strain for all of us. We had always assumed that the father of the bride would give her away. But Jane has been bitter and angry with her father and at first insisted she didn't want him there at all. But she finally gave in to the tradition.

"But I won't have that woman at my wedding!" Jane insisted.

Fortunately, Jack had the sensitivity to come without Mandy. He marched down the aisle with his daughter, stood in the reception line with me, talked and laughed and acted as if nothing had happened. I had all I could do to keep from staring at his new toupee—did approaching baldness bother him that much? Or is he trying to be as young as his girlfriend? That made me feel very middle-aged and unattractive. But I put on my smiling face, and somehow we all got through the occasion.

October 19

Because of the wedding, I didn't go to the support group meeting last week, and I'm surprised at how happy I was to see everyone again. We are entirely different kinds of people, but our common experience has bonded us together.

Tonight there was a new face. It was quite a surprise to meet Paul. A man going through the grief of divorce? They seem to be the ones who go blithely on their way, leaving the women behind holding the bag.

23

Another surprise is who he is. The Hayden's are a big name in the construction business in our city; they are also known for their participation in community affairs and their contributions to many charities. Paul is an architect who has brought that skill into the family corporation. He is a handsome, muscular man, outgoing and friendly, and his boyish grin is a lot like John's. How can he be hurting like the rest of us?

Even with my initial resistance, we women have grown quite friendly. Elsie is a coffee addict, so she comes in time to get the pot brewing, and someone usually brings doughnuts or another snack. I've had lunch with Elsie at her invitation.

Shirley's story seems to have dropped our barriers even more. Elsie has already taken Shirley under her wing. They arrived together. Tonight Elsie was ready to tell her story.

Elsie's Story

Walter never hit me, but he was constantly putting me down. My father didn't think women needed an education—they were meant to have children and belonged in the kitchen. After high school, I went to beauty school. Walter always threw it up to me that I didn't have a college education—and he did.

I liked keeping house, and I loved being a mother to my three girls. I had a small beauty shop in the basement of our home to help pay the bills. I worked hard, and sometimes I'd get very tired because Walter always wanted to go places. I remember once, when I'd settled the children for the night and hurriedly dressed, I didn't notice there was a spot on my skirt. Walter lit into me: "Just look at you! You're a mess! How can you disgrace me in front of my friends by looking this way?"

I wanted to say, "Because I'm too busy ironing your shirts and taking care of your children and earning money for your groceries," but I just clammed up and sat there quietly with all my resentment bottled up inside.

He'd say things in front of our friends like, "I wish Elsie could cook like this" (I'm really a very good cook) or "You should see the mess in my house!" And he'd get angry if I forgot to mail a letter or left a light on. Walter's always very precise and neat. I remember shortly after we were married, I had some fresh flowers and started to put them in a copper pitcher, and he laced me down. Flowers belong in vases; pitchers are for drinks. Because we couldn't afford kitchen curtains, I made some out of a set of dish towels I'd gotten at a bridal shower. I thought I'd never live that down!

Trouble is, every time Walter got angry and put me down, I'd just cringe and draw into myself. I hate scenes; I'll do anything to keep things on an even keel. It was easier to agree to his demands than to assert myself. Besides, I thought women were supposed to obey their husbands.

Once, when the girls were in high school, Rachel had a date and didn't come home until 3 a.m. I was beside myself with worry, walking the floor, and the next day I grounded her. For some reason, Walter decided to gang up on me with the girls. He said, "Your mother just doesn't understand about grown-up things because she never went to college."

After the girls were married and Walter and I were alone in the house, things got worse. "I don't love you anymore," he announced one day. "I want to live by myself." Another day he'd say, "Divorce is wrong. We need to stay together."

One day, I came home to find the doors locked. Walter was inside. I pounded on the front door and cried, "Walter, let me in!" He stood at the window and screamed, "I don't want you in my house!" I felt like a fool as I finally walked over to the neighbor's and phoned one of my daughters. "Mother," she said when she picked me up, "how long are you going to put up with this?" A few hours later when she brought me home, Walter acted as if nothing had happened.

Walter comes from a strict, German family; his father was a Lutheran minister, and his word was law in the family. No one was permitted to argue with him. When Walter was in his early teens, he was summoned to his father's office. "Well, what do you want to make of yourself?" his father asked gruffly.

"I'm not sure."

"All right, we'll make a preacher of you." And off to prep school he was sent. After his first year at the seminary, Walter decided the ministry was not for him and he quit. His father never let him forget that. In his mind, his son had failed.

I loved being in Walter's family. His mother is a jewel. Most of the time she put up with his dad's demands, but she could be spunky when she had to! Dad Becker comes across as a dignified, courtly, white-haired gentleman, and Walter would laugh with the rest of us when he would say, "Ach, that Walter! He never was a good student!" I didn't realize that inwardly he was seething.

About a year ago, we went to visit Walter's family, and Dad Becker again made some crack about Walter being a dummy, and I laughed with everyone else, but Walter just sat there and glared. On the way home, he began to harangue his father and accused me of laughing at him. As he became angrier, he drove faster and faster. I actually became afraid for my life.

We came into the house, and he started throwing things off the kitchen table. Then he grabbed the table and turned it on its side. I realized his pent-up anger was out of control. He never actually hit me, but I was afraid that at the next explosion he would.

I did what he didn't have the courage to do. I filed for divorce.

Then Paul spoke up quietly. "My wife was a victim of sexual abuse. Her father molested her. I never knew about it until last year when he died of cancer. That opened up the whole can of worms again."

That's all he said. I think he feels rather hesitant as the only man in our group of women.

October 25

I can't seem to get Elsie's story out of my mind. It's made me realize that abuse isn't always physical and how devastating verbal put-downs are. I'm having enough trouble with feelings of worthlessness without being told I'm no good.

What really bothers me is that both Shirley and Elsie have been victimized by the Bible itself. There's got to be something wrong when "obey your husband" destroys self-esteem. I took that question to Pastor Keller.

He said, "Whatever makes a person lose human dignity is a sin against the Fifth Commandment, and a spouse who submits to abuse is committing that sin. Besides, marriage is meant to be a relationship of love, not of law. Mercy and grace transcend the rules.

"We are all precious and worthwhile in God's sight. He wants to build us up, not tear us down," he continued. "Remember that, Becky, and don't be so hard on yourself either."

How did he know I've been feeling so worthless and cast-off lately?

October 27

After our meeting last night, I suggested to Elsie that we go out to lunch soon. I mentioned that I really like Mexican food but that I haven't found many people who share that taste.

"Oh, I love Mexican food," said Paul, who was standing nearby. "I'll take you to my favorite place."

"That would be fun," I said, thinking he was just making polite conversation. But this morning he called to set a date—

next Tuesday. That should be interesting! I haven't been out with a man since Jack left—except for John, of course. But John just takes me to McDonald's. That's all he can afford now that he's in college.

October 31

Paul is an excellent host and a good conversationalist. I soon learned that he really wanted to talk about his divorce but had a little trouble opening up in front of our all-female group.

Paul's Story

We've always been a close family. I get along great with my mother and father and sister, and I fit comfortably into the family business. The Hayden name is an old and prominent one in this city, and we've never had a divorce in the family. My mother is having a lot of trouble dealing with that. She keeps saying, "But Sueann is a nice girl; why can't you work things out?" It hurts me that I can't talk to her about this.

Sueann's mom lives in Florida; she's an only child. Her mother is completely passive, so when her father got cancer, Sueann was the one who put him in the hospital, paid the bills, and arranged the funeral. She handled it like a trooper, but inwardly she was very resentful, and she transferred that anger to me. Sueann has always been the passive one in our marriage; she never initiated sex. Suddenly, she became very aggressive and demanding. Other times she wouldn't let me touch her. She says I make her feel inferior because I'm successful and that I dominate her.

We live on a lake-front pretty far out in the country; I built a home on the family acreage. I love boating and golfing—the country club is practically at our doorstep. And I love the open country with the rolling hills and trees and the wildlife. Sueann is a city girl. She hates the water and doesn't golf, and unless I opened them, the shades on the windows that look down on the woods were always closed.

Sueann spends money as if it grows on trees. It doesn't seem to bother her that my success provides that. Her pastime is driving to the city and shopping. Her other obsession is our two boys. Trouble is she spoils them rotten. She buys them all the latest crazes, chauffeurs them wherever they want to go, fixes the junk food they like—no wonder Mike is overweight! I love my boys and have always tried to do father-son things with them—like my father did with me. I've tried to counteract Sueann's permissiveness, but when I do lay down the law, I'm the bad guy. I don't like that!

Now Sueann's decided to rent an apartment in the city, and she's taken up with this car salesman. She did promise she wouldn't sleep with him in front of the boys, but I'm not sure she's honored that. I know that in a divorce the mother almost always gets custody, and that worries me.

For the first time in my life, I've failed. I've failed my marriage, my boys, my parents. That's hard to take!

When he finished talking Paul said, "You know, Becky, you are a good listener. You remind me a lot of my sister, Kay. She lives in Chicago, and I really miss not having her to confide in."

So I'm a big sister—or mother-substitute. That's okay. Paul reminds me a lot of John.

November 8

I wrestle with the same feelings of failure that Paul does, and what it does to my self-esteem. Sometimes I feel I'm not fit for anything.

One of my greatest support systems has been the weekly Bible study group at our church. But I almost quit because I thought I wasn't worthy of continuing as the leader. Pastor Keller set me straight on that. "Becky," he said, "you need that

Bible class. And they need you. Even though it may not seem like it now, you're not the only one who's hurting."

I'm beginning to realize that.

Those eight women in the Bible study group have been so understanding and loving—in fact, with few exceptions, so have all my friends, even the ones who were Jack's business associates. It's been wonderful to have someone like Dave come up after church on Sunday and give me a big hug and say, "How are things with you, Becky?"

Today I took Lou home after Bible class, and she didn't get out of the car right away.

"Becky, I just want you to know that a lot of us who aren't going through a divorce don't have perfect marriages either," she said.

Lou's Story

Brad has always been a very possessive husband. He gets jealous when he thinks another man is giving me too much attention. Last Sunday, Dave and I were having an animated conversation and Dave put his hand on my arm—you know how Dave is—and Brad just stood there and glowered. In the car on the way home, he started ranting, "You didn't have to let him paw you!" I was so hurt I didn't say a word all the way home.

When we got in the house I said, "Brad, I think we have to talk."

"There's nothing to say," he said sharply. "I don't want you to ever let it happen again."

Brad wants me to be home when he's there; I haven't dared take on anything that takes me away at night. He even makes cracks about my "running off" to Bible class. I won't give that up, and he thinks I'm being very stubborn. It's okay for him to go fishing with his buddies, but turnabout is not fair play according to his way of thinking.

You know we go camping on all our vacations. That's because Brad loves to camp. I hate it!

I look at my marriage and I don't like what I see. I'm not going to walk out on Brad, but I am disappointed, very disappointed.

As she got out of the car, Lou said, "You're a good listener, Becky. Thanks for letting me get this off my chest."

That's the second time recently someone has said I'm a good listener. Is that what Pastor Keller meant when he said, "People need you"?

November 16

Tonight I shared with the support group what a blessing and support my friends are. Not all in the group have been so fortunate. One of Elsie's sisters-in-law hasn't spoken to her since her divorce.

"I thought Gloria was a good friend," mused Emily. "But every time she sees me talking to Ken, she grabs his arm and leads him away. Does she think I'm on the prowl for her husband just because I don't have one right now?"

"Shortly after Jack left," I said, "one of his business partners dropped by and suggested that he'd be happy to 'comfort me' when I needed it. I was so shocked I just said, 'No, thank you!' and ushered him to the door. Do some men think they are God's gift to women? Or that divorced women are so sex-starved that they'll take up with anyone?"

"Carl keeps coming around and saying we should have sex," said Emily. " 'Until the divorce is final, we're still married,' he says. I wanted it so bad I gave in a couple of times, but afterwards I felt cheap and used. It's no good!"

"How do you all feel about sex?" asked Marcia. "And abstinence?"

"Sometimes I miss it so much I'd be tempted to go to bed with any man who asked me," admitted Emily. "I don't want to face the rest of my life without a man."

"Perhaps you won't have to," said Marcia. "It may seem distasteful to you now, but a good percentage of divorcees do remarry."

"Oh, I could never remarry," said Elsie. "That would be a sin."

We looked at her in surprise.

"It says so in the Bible: 'Whoever divorces and marries another commits adultery.' I got the divorce. So if I married again I would be committing adultery."

"Did you get the divorce because you wanted to marry someone else?" asked Marcia.

"Of course not."

"Elsie, my dear," explained Marcia patiently, "filing for divorce does not mean you are the guilty party. That was a legal step for your protection."

"Besides," I said, "Pastor Keller says there is only one unpardonable sin, and it's not divorce! He's helped me realize how loving and forgiving God is and that He always gives us a chance for a new beginning."

I'm not sure we persuaded Elsie or eased her guilt completely. Her father-in-law keeps writing some pretty judgmental letters, and her children are trying to patch up their parent's marriage.

For me, sexual abstinence isn't as hard as living without that 'other.' It's as if Jack and I were joined at the hip and have been surgically separated, and the wound hurts. Having someone put his arm around me, snuggling up close, reaching over from my side of the bed to know someone is there—I miss that the most!

That's one reason I enjoy going out to lunch with Paul. It feels so good to have a man open the car door and escort me to our table, to be a male-female entity in a society where that's the norm. Paul's taking me out for Chinese food next week. I guess he needs to talk to an older sister again.

Paul is not regular in attending our support group meetings, but he's a gregarious man and seems to like our company when he does come. Last week he was talking to Marcia about golf and offered to give her some lessons.

November 30

John was home for Thanksgiving last week, and Jack didn't come around to take him golfing. When I mentioned that, he said, "Well, it's getting late in the season, and I guess Dad is pretty busy." But he didn't look at me when he spoke, and I could tell that he was hurt.

So I asked Jane what was going on. "It's Mandy, Mother. She's jealous of us. She tries to keep Dad from seeing us. But I won't stand for it!"

Jane's anger has transferred to Jack's paramour. She's always been sympathetic of the underdog, and she sees her father as a victim of Mandy's possessiveness. Suddenly, she's very protective of him and delights in spiriting him away for clandestine father-daughter lunches. I question her motives, but I'm glad she's made peace with her father.

Last week at lunch, Paul talked about his youngest son who is having fights with all of his friends. He's also overeating and becoming tubbier.

Tonight Emily told us that her oldest child is having bad dreams and nightmares and that she hangs on to her and cries when she leaves for work.

I'm beginning to see that the ramifications of divorce go much farther than the separation of two people. It's like a rock thrown into the water—the ripples spread out to the family, relatives, friends—so many people are affected in one way or another.

My adult children are by no means unscathed either.

December 4

Bob Johnson, my lawyer, called his morning. The divorce hearing is set for December 22. I'm sure Jack is delighted. He can give Mandy her wedding for Christmas!

Bob says I don't have to be in court when the divorce is finalized. Jack has been so anxious to marry Mandy that he's very generous. Sometimes I think I'd like to really clean him out, but there's no point in being vindictive, and I know I have too much pride to accept support from a man I'm not married to! So I've just asked for the house and a cash settlement for its upkeep and the court costs. The children have their trust funds, and as long as Jack pays John's college tuition, I'll get by.

But what a Christmas present for me! Looking forward to the holidays seemed bleak enough—and now this! I wish I could just run away for that week.

December 7

I've received an invitation from my brother Dan to come to Nebraska for Christmas, and I'm sorely tempted to accept. I hate to leave the children without either parent—we've always made such a family celebration of Christmas—but I don't know if I can bear to trim a tree and bake and decorate in this lonely house.

Jane is urging me to go. She's so excited about her and Zach sharing their first Christmas together, and she's promised to look after John and include him in their plans. I'm sure she'd love to go through my ornaments and decorations and use what their little apartment has room for. Maybe this is the Lord's way of helping me through another difficult time.

December 14

Tonight the support group commiserated with the news of my upcoming divorce hearing. Perhaps I'm just numb, but I'm not that upset. Actually, right now I have a feeling of relief, as if a chapter in my life is finally ending. My future isn't what I wanted or planned, but I might as well get on with it.

I've decided to go back to full-time work after Christmas. There's always a demand for night nurses. Working that shift helps me get through the loneliest hours and gives me time to continue my church activities. It's not going to be easy to adjust to a smaller income, but I haven't always had such a high standard of living—I can manage.

I guess I'm fortunate at that. Emily is having a rough go of it. She's trying to keep her aerobics class along with her full-time accounting job, and she's barely squeaking by. Her parents help when they can, particularly with the children. But she's had to hire a part-time baby-sitter. No wonder she always looks so tired and harried.

Poor Shirley is completely destitute and helpless. She's staying with her husband's sister right now, but the family's limited means and small house don't make her feel welcome. "I know I need to find something else," she said, "but right now I don't know where to turn."

Elsie's problem is handling bills and insurance and tax forms and household repairs; even balancing a checkbook is something she hasn't done before. "Walter handled all the money," she said. "I charged the supplies for my beauty shop and turned the receipts over to him; he took care of all the bills and investments. I had a weekly allowance for groceries and clothing, and that was it."

But I have to admire her guts. The first thing she did was to buy a used car and take driving lessons. "At first I was terrified at having all that responsibility myself," she added. "I made a lot of mistakes, and sure, some tradesmen took advantage of me. But I'm getting by, and that makes me feel good about myself."

January 4, 1990

Christmas was a journey back into my childhood! We went to the Christmas Eve service at the church where Dan's children helped tell the beautiful story of Jesus' birth. Christmas Day we were at Uncle Ed and Aunt May's farmhouse for a huge, old-fashioned turkey dinner. Mother and I had some wonderful private visits. And it snowed! For a few days, I was Rebecca Jane Schneider again—not Becky Carlson, newly divorced.

But as the plane neared Los Angeles, I began to feel more and more as if a weight were pulling me down. I'm right back in the old cycle of working as hard as I can to forget my loneliness, and then coming home exhausted to an empty house and not liking it. I wonder if I'll ever get used to it! So much for nostalgia!

I continue to marvel at the way Marcia handles our support

group. She doesn't say much, but her gentle questions help us express our feelings about what is happening in our lives. I can see how she has guided us through the stages of grief: depression, denial, anger, guilt, low self-esteem. I know the final step is acceptance—I've read Kubler-Ross. I'm not there yet.

Marcia's divorce is farther in the past, and she seems to be fulfilled and happy. When I remarked to her that she had her act so well together, she looked at me strangely. "Becky," she said, "you will learn that there is life after divorce."

"But," she added, "the scars are there."

January 17

Recently I read an article in a magazine about men in midlife crisis, and as the symptoms were described, every one of them fit Jack! I realized how terrified he has always been of getting older and how many ploys he used to deny the process even before Mandy came into the picture. I remembered how upset he was at me for throwing a 40th birthday party for him. I look on middle-age as another chapter in my life, and so I didn't really understand or sympathize with his fears.

I thought they were over, but here I am again with these feelings of guilt and failure. I should have seen what was right under my nose; perhaps I could have done something to make Jack feel more secure about his aging.

So I talked to Pastor Keller again.

"Becky," he said, "do you believe God has forgiven you?"

"Of course I do."

"Then isn't it time you forgave yourself?"

That pulled me up short. He's right! It's time to put the past to rest.

"And it's time for you to forgive Jack," he continued. "He needs God's forgiveness every bit as much as you do. And he needs you to give it to him."

Have I forgiven Jack? I think so. Mandy has weaned him away from most of our mutual friends, so our paths don't often cross. He continues to be prosperous. He and Mandy live in a large, modern ranch house, and he drives a Nissan 300ZX.

Mandy wears expensive (and for my taste) gaudy clothes; she's gotten even heavier since the baby was born. I have a feeling that her dependence and possessiveness are beginning to wear a bit thin, and that Jack is realizing he's a bit old to be the father of a small daughter. He doesn't look happy, and I really do feel sorry for him.

But I'm not quite ready to face him and say, "Jack, I forgive you." I'll have to do more praying about that.

January 28

The sermon this morning was about Joseph and his brothers, and Pastor Keller brought out that God can take the bad things that happen in our lives and bring good from them. My divorce was a bad thing. I'm sure God didn't want my marriage to end either. But I can see His guidance and healing. I know I am a more patient, sympathetic person than I was six months ago.

There's a plaque on the wall in pastor's study that reads, "Please be patient with me. God isn't finished with me yet."

That's me! I'm not okay yet—but I'm getting there!

Epilog

December 18, 1991

Last week I ran into Paul at the bookstore for the first time in almost two years, and he suggested we have lunch again to catch up on what's been happening in our lives.

"I guess you know Marcia and I have been dating," he said. "And we'll probably be getting married soon. Marcia's first marriage ended because she was successful in her career and her husband was a failure. That's not true for us, and even though our areas of expertise are completely different, we find a lot to talk about and enjoy challenging and learning from each other. We're not rushing things; we've both been burned once, and we're still a little scared."

So I came home and dug out this journal and reread the saga of the first six months of my divorce.

Our support group has long gone their separate ways. I still have lunch with Elsie, and she has kept in touch with everyone. Emily is married to another divorcee who has custody of his three children—it's a good thing she was stuck with that big house! So far two families and seven children under one roof seem to be working.

Elsie took Shirley into her home while she completed a course in computer operation. Now Shirley is able to support herself and has her own apartment. She hasn't remarried; neither has Elsie.

Nor have I. I've had a few dates and enjoy being in the company of a man, but I haven't found anyone special yet. Perhaps I never will; there aren't that many unmatched men my age out there. But I am content. I have learned to live with what the Lord has given me and to wait patiently for His next step. Meanwhile, I've organized a divorce support group at our church.

John is out of college and has a job in Texas, so I sold our big house and bought a smaller condominium. My greatest joy these days is my grandson Josh. "I don't know how I'm going to tell him he has a step-aunt who's only two years older than he is," laughs Jane.

I did finally have the opportunity to talk to Jack alone and to tell him that I forgave him. It wasn't as hard as I thought it would be. He looked at me quietly and said, "Thank you, Becky. I do appreciate that."

As for me, saying those words brought a great sense of relief—as if the finish of this chapter of my life has finally been written.

Marcia is right. There is life after divorce.

But the scars remain.

An Encouraging Word

One husband leaves his wife and moves in with a younger woman carrying his child. A second pushed his physically weaker partner down the stairs killing their unborn baby. A third locks his wife out of the house and is psychologically abusive to her. A fourth chooses booze and a motorcycle in place of maturity, responsibility, and children. A wife uses her children and her husband's paycheck to fulfill her own narcissistic needs without even an appreciative glance towards the hardworking man she pledged to love forever.

Victims abound in Rebecca's story, victims of circumstance, victims of the times, victims of a "me generation" society. Being burned once (and in real life, for some people, two times or more), it would be easy to live out the rest of one's life in a depressive, bitter state. This is neither Rebecca's choice nor God's plan for her life. Before discussing Rebecca's journey of faith, it seems appropriate to digress for a moment to consider some thoughts regarding marriage and divorce in general.

Camelot

Jane marries Zach. Rebecca marries Jack. Paul marries Sueann. Paul marries Marcia. Beginning a marriage holds so much promise: the wedding plans, the happy and excited family and friends, the first apartment, the first piece of furniture, the first house, the first child—many dreams, many expectations, many goals. The possibilities seem endless. Hope and "love" abound.

As the years go by, reality confronts fantasy. The dreams and expectations begin to pale in the light of the routine and responsibility of day-to-day living. The possibilities seem to fade. If the commitment, the heart of the marriage, is no longer intact, then the bonding between the couple, as human beings, as husband and wife, begins to unravel.

The husband no longer loves and sacrifices for his wife as Christ loved the church and gave Himself up for His bride. The wife no longer feels she can submit herself to her husband. A void in the interaction is evident. The marriage is no longer under the protective wing of God our Father. One of the partners has stepped out from under this protective canopy. One of the partners has decided not to honor the lifelong commitment he or she made in God's presence with His blessing.

> What God has joined together, let no man put asunder.

> I now pronounce you husband and wife in the name of the Father and of the Son and of the Holy Spirit.

What happened to the hopes and dreams, the joys and expectations? Are satisfying marriages possible or just a mirage for the newlyweds?

Components of a Successful Christian Marriage Relationship

Successful marriages do exist. There are definite signals and signs that earmark a successful Christian marriage and a healthy, functional relationship. These components can be used in a practical way by a Christian woman to take the pulse of her marriage. They can also help her evaluate whether she is doing her part in maintaining a healthy marital relationship.

1. *Both partners are willing to submit themselves to God, His will, and His ways.* God's Law and Gospel are active in their lives. They acknowledge their own sinfulness and rely on God's mercy. They are willing to love each other as God in Christ has loved them. They are willing to forgive one another as God has forgiven them.

2. *Both partners are willing to commit themselves to the marriage and to each other.* Marriage is hard work. The marriage ceremony does not end the courtship process; it merely moves it along. Spouses change over the years. The meaning of the commitment must be reassessed to keep the marriage current. In successful marriages, both partners recommit themselves to entering each new stage of life with their beloved.

3. *Both partners are willing to be emotionally open and to stay emotionally open, revealing the very core of who they are to the other.* This is a risk-taking behavior that could result in rejection. Manifesting oneself to one's partner takes courage and a basic trust that the other person will not use revealed weaknesses to overpower and control. Often Christians need to remind themselves that they have been created, redeemed, and sanctified by God Himself. They need to remember they are each unique creations. They need to take heart and not be afraid to be all that God intended.

4. *Both partners are willing to take the time to get to know each other.* To know one another in a marriage relationship is to know the other in the most intimate of all ways. There is no other relationship quite the same. This is the only relationship where a person knows the other in the biblical sense of Genesis 4:1. To know another sexually, to know how, when, where, and what pleases the other sexually is a knowledge reserved only for the marriage relationship. To know intimate details of another's psyche is part of being in this close relationship. The partners must learn what the other needs to survive physically, psychologically, and spiritually. Both will take time and effort to find out the daily dreams and expectations of their partner. It is important to know what excites and holds the interest of the other and what pushes his or her buttons in a negative sense. To know another as intimately as couples do in marriage is to have a lot of power over the other. This knowledge can be used for good or

evil, to put down or build up the self-esteem of the other.
5. *Both partners cultivate the ability to accept the differences of their partner without trying to remold or recreate what God has created and called good.* Changes in personality and behavior are possible but only if the partner desires to make a change. Nagging never works.
6. *Both partners need to balance their mutual resources so that the basic survival needs of both parties are being met and each can continue to dream dreams and set new goals.* Goals need to be realistic and specific. Each partner should be able to see some of his or her dreams come to fruition.
7. *Both partners will take their requests to God. They pray for their spouse and the marriage relationship.* There is power and strength beyond our expectation that is available when we approach our Father, who lavishes us with spiritual gifts. "Ask and it will be given to you; seek and you will find; knock and the door will be opened to you. For everyone who asks receives; he who seeks finds; and to him who knocks, the door will be opened" (Luke 11:9–10 NIV).

Breaking the Commitment to God

When one or the other partner walks out from under the umbrella of God's love and also steps outside the circle of God's Law, the chances of that marriage succeeding decrease significantly. The rules of the game have changed. God is no longer central. Self-centered personal ethics take over. The Ten Commandments no longer apply. It becomes acceptable to covet our neighbor's spouse. It becomes acceptable to have an affair. It may even become acceptable to beat a wife, hurt or harm her body, or break her spirit with words. Outside the Christian faith, there is no conscious need of God's forgiveness, no repentance, no change in behavior. There is no honoring of the marriage vows, no commitment to loving God, husband, or wife. When this commitment to the partner stops, the marriage comes to a grinding halt. The marriage is between two parties. If only one person remains committed, it is not a marriage. It will not work.

Rebecca's Journey of Faith

Becky experienced the problem of one-sided commitment. Becky is one of the blessed women of God going through a divorce. Jack stated that Becky was a strong woman and would survive without him. Becky's thoughts and emotions, her grappling with the grieving process, make Jack's words ring true. Becky demonstrates a great deal of both internal ego strength and external behavioral control.

Becky allows us a glimpse into her inner world, into her heart. We feel her pain and despair as she mourns the death of her marriage, but we also are aware of her strengths, her defenses, her coping mechanisms, and her faith. We see her go through the grieving process: the shock, the denial, the guilt, the bargaining, the anger, the depression, the false hope, and finally, the acceptance.

Becky quickly takes stock of her resources, probably on a subconscious level, and takes action. She is a woman of action. She uses her unique God-given personality to tackle this unexpected life crisis. She uses the same method she has used to tackle many smaller problems in her life. She has her own style of coping, and it works. She reaches within for whatever strength she can find. She reaches to God to add to her own reserve. She reaches out to her family, friends, and pastor for additional support.

Family and Friends

Becky is very open about her thoughts, feelings, and needs with her children and her friends. Although she was in shock and denial for a time and hid the truth of her broken marriage even from herself, she eventually perceives her family and friends to be part of a safe and user-friendly environment. It is interesting to note that Becky doesn't even comment on her own openness. For Becky it appears to be a very natural, normal, and healthy way to work through disappointment. Besides sharing, receiving feedback from others is part of her style of relating. Her friends and family label her a good listener. She labels herself as a good listener. She is able to digest new information. It is natural for her to think that her children, her friends, and even Jack will have thoughts and emotions different from hers. She is a very strong, emotionally healthy, Christian woman.

Becky's friend Judy assertively urges Becky to go to a Christian divorce group. Becky seems to have an internal drive moving her towards health and healing. But even strong individuals like Becky are never totally stalwart. Instinctively she sensed her own weakness and her own need for help and for others to lean on as she worked through her grief. Because of the shock of her husband leaving so suddenly and because of the depressive portion of the grieving process, Becky needed a push, a helpful hint, a suggestion to help propel her forward in the healing process. Her internal energy supply was low. She needed to hear about the divorce recovery group from someone like Judy. She chose to listen to Judy's suggestion and to follow through with it.

Divorce Recovery Group

Anyone who has attended group therapy sessions or a divorce recovery group can identify with Becky's initial anxiety. Becky's journal describes her first reaction of withdrawal and hesitation about sharing her thoughts with strangers. As Becky develops empathy with the other group members, she gains the courage to share her story and to receive support from others. Becky is grateful for Marcia, who leads the group gently through the stages of grief and through the healing process.

Pastor Keller

For Becky, the healing process also included reaching out to Pastor Keller with special areas of concern. Becky turns to her pastor for guidance in dealing with her guilt, her need for God's forgiveness, and her inability to forgive Jack. Becky did not appear to get stuck at any one juncture. The five months of journal entries show her moving through her emotions in a healthy manner at a normal rate of speed. The final stage of forgiving Jack marked an ending to this spiritual journey for Becky.

Coping Mechanisms

In the beginning when the pain was great, Becky demonstrates the ability to step aside and find temporary respite and relief from the intensity of the pain. She knits three sweaters. This coping mechanism helped. Becky puts on a painted smile, a mask, for while. She continues to work and to lead her weekly Bible study group. At first Becky tells no one that Jack is gone. The issue is too devastating to share. Becky travels back to Nebraska and re-experiences the nostalgia of pre-marriage Christmases of the past. She has a moment of respite. With each one of these coping mechanisms, Becky temporarily sets aside the terrible pain in a healthy way.

Facing the Pain

But Becky always goes back to the pain and faces straight on what she needs to face. She experiences and goes through her feelings. She has an inner strength and a subconscious confidence that God will see her through this day, this hour, this time. She trusts that there will be another more tolerable emotion on another day sometime in the future. She has the courage to let the pain come. In the very beginning, when she allows herself to experience the pain, she has no words to even express the depth of her despair. She has no words to describe her helplessness. She curls up in a ball and groans, aware of God's presence, God's care and concern for her as one of His children.

Facing Mandy

Becky shows amazing emotional maturity and self-control when she accidently runs into Jack and the pregnant Mandy. Becky maintains emotional control and remains socially appropriate throughout the surprise encounter. Becky's behavior was similar at Jane's wedding. Becky found it emotionally tense but socially acceptable to interact with Jack during the festivities.

Growth Experiences

As time marches on, Becky seems to turn this whole experience around and begins to see it as a growth experience. Her world expands as she listens to the stories of others in the divorce group. She vicariously experiences the feelings of the others whose lives were intruded upon by spouses demonstrating behaviors outside of God's covenant. She sees the havoc raised when one spouse unilaterally decides to put God's covenant aside and to follow his or her own desires with no regard for God or the other. She witnesses the effects of physical, sexual, and emotional abuse. She sees the cause-effect relationship when the commandments a loving God intends for the good of human beings are broken. Becky experiences and hears about the devastation that occurs when one person is bonded to the marriage and the other is not. She sees what happens when Genesis 2:24 is ignored, when a husband no longer cleaves to his wife and is no longer committed unto her as one flesh.

The Marriage Bond

Learning to cleave or cling to a spouse in marriage with appropriate intensity starts in early childhood. Children learn to trust and bond to their parents first. They slowly transfer that ability to bond to others. The bonding that occurs between parent and child and husband and wife has many similar basic elements, including trust and respect for the other. If that original bond were never formed or if it were damaged or broken along the way, the child has been wounded. Children hurt by abuse, neglect, or abandonment by one or both parents normally have a deep wound. For some, the infection and the scar tissue may prevent them from forming healthy, intimate relationships as adults without the help of a therapist. Divorce is often perceived by children as abandonment, as trauma. Even court-ordered visitation can add to the feeling of abandonment if a young child is separated from the primary caretaker for any length of time.

Christians Sin

Christian men and women make mistakes. Some of these mistakes are indeed sins. Sin breaks our relationship with God. His forgiveness is necessary to restore us. Jack is a Christian who has made a very serious error in judgment. His life has changed also. His behavior has resulted in lifelong consequences. Becky observed that he did not look all that happy.

Problems Multiply

Many people have a much more difficult time with divorce recovery than Becky and the people mentioned in her journal. For many others, the problems during divorce recovery multiply and answers seem impossible. For many, their income level and life-style change dramatically. For many, there is no support system, no understanding family, friends, pastor, or divorce recovery group. For many who have ongoing problems with relationships, bonding, and stress, the wounds stay open and gaping. Many need treatment for these open wounds, but because of lack of courage or resources, they pretend all is well and go on. The wounds may appear healed on the surface, but the deepest part of the wounds, if untreated, may stay unstitched and heal improperly. These wounds will fester and cause problems later on.

Health and Hope

Psychological and self-help material on divorce recovery abounds. There is a wealth of material written on relationships and how to communicate with one another in a healthy manner. There is material written for those whose ability to bond and attach was damaged in childhood or youth. Informed pastors and counselors can be helpful in adding support and encouragement or can assist by referring a person to another professional who can act as a guide and coach during the healing process. Human beings can learn again how to relate to others in a functional, healthy manner. As they heal, they can once again feel the warmth and love that only a child of God, bonded to Him, experiences. As they heal, they can also pass on support, encouragement, and healing to others. Becky also became a blessing to other divorced individuals when she started a divorce recovery group at her church.

Life is different after a divorce, sometimes even better. The pretending and denial finally stop. Life changes. Life goes on. To quote Marcia, "There is life after divorce. But the scars remain."

Most scars fade over time. The Gospel heals. Beginning life after divorce can be difficult. It also can be an adventure. It takes courage. It is possible to dream dreams again. It is possible to set new goals and expectations. Hope and love can again abound. It is a new stage of life, a new beginning, a new opportunity given to Becky and the other divorce survivors who know an ascended Savior who continues to hold up His hands of blessing, scars and all.

Shirley Schaper

Reflection

- If you are married, what do you think contributes to the success/failure of your marriage? What parts do trust, respect, commitment, and forgiveness play in human relationships, especially marriage?
- What does Ephesians 5 say to you about God's design for Christian life and love, especially as it relates to marriage and family?
- If you have experienced divorce, how was your personal journey the same or different from Becky's? What helped you cope? How have you seen yourself going through the stages of the grieving process (shock, denial, guilt, bargaining, anger, depression, false hope, acceptance)?
- What experiences have you had with support groups similar to Becky's? What value do you see in sharing personal experiences and struggles with people in both similar and different situations? Note Galations 6:1–5.
- Facing the pain of divorce can be very difficult. Part of the pain may be admitting your own part in the failure of your marriage. How would you have responded if Pastor Keller said to you, as he did to Becky, "You are guilty"?
- How does Luke 6:37–38 help friends and family members shape their attitudes toward those experiencing divorce?
- If you are a divorce survivor, what advice would you share with others going through a similar experience?

Dear God,
You are there
when I don't even have words
to describe the pain I feel.

You are there
in the people who love me
and listen to me
and challenge me
and encourage me.

You are there
when I can honestly say
I was wrong.
When I can honestly say
I forgive him.
I forgive her.

You are there,
putting me together,
shaping and reshaping me,
and lifting me
with new life.

Thank You!

Amen.

Story 2

Kim: All Things New

by Lauren Beale

Kim

"Jessica Leigh, I baptize you in the name of the Father and of the Son and of the Holy Spirit."

Those words that your father spoke only a few hours ago constantly replay in my mind as I hold you close and feed you tonight. A few hours ago, we thought you might die—we weren't sure how your tiny body would handle the dyes and sedatives the doctors said you'd have to have in order for the CT and bone scans to be done. Plus your apnea monitor had to be off during the scans. And if you were okay through these tests, would what they'd find be life-threatening?

Your father and I were scared, so we called again upon God and His mercy and healing power. Sometimes it seems that's all we've been doing for the last 19 days—the first 19 days of your life, my little firstborn child. How could any childbirth class or conversation with other new parents ever have prepared us for this odd, confusing, frustrating, tear-filled yet miraculous 19-day timespan. All we can do is rely on God's promises and cherish the prayers of His people.

Everything I've heard and read says this is an emotional and tiring time for a new mother—my hormones are supposed to be goofy. Sometimes I've secretly wished that was all that was going on—that we could be a "normal" family adjusting to our new roles as your parents. Evidently God had other ideas. Your life already sounds like a soap opera.

We wanted you so badly. Finally, with the aid of an infertility specialist, I did become pregnant. But by the time we shared the good news, I was already bleeding and miscarrying. The good news for us was I could become pregnant again.

Five months later, you were conceived, Jess. We were so excited. The pregnancy went great. I didn't even have morning sickness like poor Cathy next door. At four months, Dr. Marshall took your picture for us during an ultrasound. We proudly showed it to friends and relatives pointing out your face and hands. They tried to visualize you as best as possible, but the photo just wasn't the same as seeing you move on the TV screen. Each appointment, each movement and kick you made, every childbirth class was a major event in our lives. Friends were probably tired of our descriptions but patiently listened. As your due date approached, Dad refinished a chest of drawers and painted the room. I put up the Noah's ark wallpaper border. We bought the crib and had everything we thought you'd need in place.

Finally my doctor's appointments were to begin weekly instead of biweekly. Cathy came home with her firstborn—Joshua David—and I got to hold him. (She had gotten pregnant so easily and only had eight hours of labor.) A few hours later, 12:21 a.m. to be exact, I awoke to an odd sensation. I thought labor had begun, but I wasn't sure; the pains didn't agree with what we'd been taught—they were all in front. Two hours later, I woke up your dad. The quiet, gentle phrase, "Bruce, I think I'm in labor, but I'm not sure" got an immediate response. "How far apart are the contractions? When did it start? Are you packed? Should I call the hospital?" He was excited but obviously shocked that the doctor's predictions could be so far off. We waited. The regular contractions continued but still didn't follow the "pattern" described in childbirth classes. When they reached five minutes apart, your father called the hospital. "Childbirth classes give you guidelines, but not everyone is the same. It sounds like your wife is in labor; bring her in," the nurse responded.

We quickly packed (How was I to know you'd be three weeks early?) and moved as fast as contractions and 35 extra pounds would allow until I got into the car. The seven-minute drive to the hospital was uncomfortable to say the least, but there's very little traffic that early in the morning.

After being weighed, questioned, changed into a hospital gown, and checked by a nurse and a resident, it was agreed—you were on your way. I was in medium to hard labor, a position I'd stay in for the next 17 hours. You were hooked up to an internal monitor. With that and an IV in place, trips to the rest room were the only walking I was allowed to do. While I knew every feature of the birthing room, I could have cared less where I was. All I knew was that the lady in the next room had her baby and my substitute doctor went home for dinner. (Dr. Marshall didn't think you'd be born this soon and left town for the weekend.) Because labor continued but dilation stopped, I was given pitocin to induce harder labor. But it was introduced too rapidly and had to be stopped. When Dr. Olsen returned, it was started again. This time it worked, and you began the last part of your trip into this world. Just as I thought it would soon be over, the doctor declared you were stuck and decided to use forceps. I will never forget the pain of him pressing on my stomach with each push while he held you with the forceps. But after 21 hours of labor, at 9:21 p.m., you were placed into my arms for the first time. You smiled. And it was all worthwhile—love at first sight.

After your first family photos were taken, Dad started the phone calls telling everyone you had arrived. He was so proud! "Yes, we've already inspected, and she has 10 fingers and 10 toes and lots of dark hair."

I guess you didn't need to hear all of this; after all, you were there. But I've been told new moms have this insatiable desire to tell all the details to everyone. And I guess they're right.

Well anyway, they eventually came and took you for tests and observation. Dad and I moved to my semi-private room and ate box lunches (the first meal I'd had all day). The nurses promised to bring you in for feedings throughout the night since we decided on breast-feeding. Dad said goodnight and headed home. I said a simple prayer of thanks and dozed off, exhausted from the day's events.

Sunlight flooded my room by the time I woke up. The nurse arrived to check on me. "We'll bring your baby in as soon as Dr. Schmidt has had a chance to talk to you," she stated and left the room leaving me to eat breakfast and wonder what was wrong.

"Good morning. Have you seen Jessica yet this morning?" Dr. Schmidt's cheery greeting as he strolled across the room and sat down did little to calm the unsettled feeling I had after the nurse's visit. I was still glad we had chosen him as our pediatrician.

"No, the nurse said you'd talk to me first."

"Well, Jessica had a few problems while she was being observed last night. She stopped breathing several times; the longest period was 23 seconds. Other than the apnea she seems quite healthy. Just to be safe, we've placed her on a monitor that you'll have to keep on her around the clock for at least three months. If you have any questions, I'll be happy to answer them at any time. The nurses will show you all you need to know about the monitor."

My mind was inundated with questions. I had never even heard of apnea. Would you be all right? What does this mean for the future? What happens after three months? In the midst of my questions, Dr. Marshall arrived. "Oh, it's more important that you talk to Dr. Schmidt now," he said. "But don't worry, my son went home on a monitor too. It came off after three months and he's fine now. I'll stop back later." He was gone.

Dr. Schmidt answered each question, but I'm not sure much was actually sinking in. All I wanted to do was to hold you and call your daddy. "I'll be back later to talk to both you and Bruce," Dr. Schmidt reassured me. "Here's Jessica now."

You were hungry, but the monitor, with lights flashing whenever you breathed and when your heart beat, was intimidating. "It's okay to pick her up," the nurse encouraged. But as I did the monitor squealed like someone scraping her fingernails on a chalkboard. Other nurses knew the signal and came running. "When it's a constant squeal like this it simply means the leads have shifted. If it were an emergency and you needed to start CPR on Jessica, you would hear beeps at one-second intervals. Let's start over again," the nurse suggested as we adjusted the strap around your chest and reset the monitor.

With the nurses' help, you and I finally got settled and eventually learned and felt comfortable with breast-feeding. Look at you now; you're growing well, eating well, and you've set a definite time schedule—every two hours throughout the night. Will I ever know what it's like to sleep all night again and actually feel rested?

Well, the next day and a half were filled with feeding, snuggling with you, and talking with visitors and on the phone. Dad and I attended a car-seat safety class and learned to care for you and me. I rested but only a little bit. I was too excited to accept what others said was best for me. Besides, I felt great and was running on nervous energy. We watched hospital videos, made trips to the bathroom, and learned infant CPR. Dad and I both had to learn infant CPR before they'd let us take you home. We were told anyone who baby-sits while you're on the monitor must know this procedure as well.

We were adjusting and enjoying being a family despite the added stress of living with the apnea monitor until they told me a test hadn't worked properly and we'd have to leave you in the hospital an extra day. I'd have to go home without you. I felt like my world had ended. I couldn't leave my baby! We stayed as late as we were allowed and then tearfully said goodbye to you as they wheeled me out of the maternity ward to our car.

"You can call anytime," the nurses said. "You should be able to take her home tomorrow."

The evening's fear and frustration were overpowered by joy when the hospital called at 7 a.m. "Come pick up your child. Last night's test went well," the voice said. Finally, after getting you dressed and fed, collecting your free baby product samples, and signing papers for the monitor, we were accompanied to our Volkswagen—a family of three. The sun shone brightly on August 5th as Dad took our homecoming picture on the front porch. We rejoiced at being home together. We'd finally be able to be a normal family.

But God's timing was different than ours. The joys of watching you discover your fingers and jam them into your toothless mouth and spending time rocking and singing to you were overshadowed by your diarrhea and a bruise that was spreading across your right eyelid.

Neighbors, friends, and grandparents visited and brought presents for you. Daddy's parents were so thoughtful. Even though they traveled four and a half hours to meet you, brought meals for us, and helped with whatever we needed done, they stayed in a nearby motel so we wouldn't have the added stress of extra people in the house while we were adjusting as a family. I think the most fun visitor though was your great-grandfather who grinned and lovingly cooed at you each time he held you.

Daddy took an active part in caring for you—proving that real men do change diapers. But he convinced me to switch from cloth to disposable diapers after being soaked by you even though you were triple diapered. We tried cancelling the diaper service but it had been a gift. Oh well, I guess you'll have a lot of clean cloths to spit up on, and I won't have as much laundry to do for the next few months.

By your first weekend home, I convinced Dad we needed to get out. He took us to an area shopping mall where we could leisurely walk in air-conditioned comfort. You slept in the front baby carrier sack next to my tummy. Inquisitive shoppers strained to see the tiny baby I carried. One couple, however, scolded us for taking such a young child out of the house. Little did they know I was the one suffering from overexertion on this excursion, not you. I didn't appreciate their advice but smiled tiredly and politely thanked them and said we'd be returning home soon. Dad almost had to carry both of us to the car. It was a good thing he had taken some time off of work to help us out at home.

It had felt good to be out for a few hours, but by evening I was tired and looked forward to a reasonable night's sleep. Unfortunately, you were up and grouchy all night. The hot summer night in our unair-conditioned home probably didn't help. Daddy moved us to the spare bed in the basement. It was cooler, but it didn't have much effect on your disposition.

Sunday we took you to church for the first time. As worshipers gathered around you, we warned the pastor that if your monitor squealed during the sermon, it wasn't a reflection on the content, and we'd drop the sound as quickly as possible. Even though we were tired, I guess we were getting our sense of humor back. The bright-colored banners swaying in the breeze, the lights, and the music seemed to interest you. It felt good to be among friends, but I was inwardly relieved that, with the monitor on, you couldn't easily be passed from person to person. For now most would have to be content with viewing you in your child carrier sitting on the church pew.

Monday's doctor's appointment confirmed you had picked up rotovirus in the hospital. I guess you had a reason for having diarrhea and for being grouchy Saturday night. We'd have to be careful so it didn't spread to the other infants in our circle of friends. You had lost weight, but your bruise was still growing. "Some people may even joke about child abuse with that black eye," Dr. Schmidt commented. "We know that's not the case, so let's watch the bruise carefully."

As if that appointment hadn't been enough, flashing lights appeared in my rear view mirror on the way home. "I was being so careful. What could I possibly have done wrong," I whined inwardly. As soon as I pulled the car over, you started to cry and hold your breath between screams. The monitor started beeping off the seconds, and now a policeman wanted to know if we had renewed our license plates. Why me, Lord? A check of state computer records proved we had paid. Who knows where the stickers went. Daddy picked up replacements on the way home. All I could think of was "Lord, You promised never to give me more than I can handle, so why do I feel like I'm far past that point? Help!"

The monitor had become my friend and gave me the comfort needed so I could rest when you did (as long as the phone didn't ring), without having to worry about Sudden Infant Death Syndrome. If you stopped breathing, that squeal would wake up anyone! We looked for joy in simple things.

Tuesday your umbilical cord fell off. Now we could give you a real bath. Wednesday the public health nurse came to answer any questions I had and to check you over. You'd regained six and one-half ounces. By Friday you were back up to your birth weight, but the bruise was still spreading.

Daddy and I tearfully followed doctor's orders and admitted you to Children's Hospital for tests and your second night away from us since you were born. You were discharged the next morning with glowing test results. The nurse was happy for us but disappointed too. She had hoped to be able to give you—one of the few healthy babies she cared for—a bath.

We took you home, and as Daddy took pictures, I gave you your first real bath in a baby bathtub. You loved the water! Maybe we'll make it as parents yet.

Tuesday morning your hunger cry woke me at 5:50 a.m. What a startling surprise—you and I both slept for almost seven hours! God knew I would need that sleep to help me through the doctor's phone call later that morning. "We've consulted with some specialists and want you to take Jessica back to Children's Hospital tomorrow for a CT scan and a bone scan. There is some risk involved, but her bruise is probably an indication that she has a tumor," he reported.

Long-distance conversations with a Christian friend who is also a neurosurgeon and lots of prayer led us to the conclusion that, for your sake, we had no choice—we had to go through with the tests.

Bright and early this morning we again checked you into Children's Hospital and were directed to the room for your bone scan—Children's Hospital Room 323. That's where you were baptized.

The technologists told us that infants were hard to keep

totally still for the scan so you'd have to be sedated. Your monitor would have to be removed during the procedure too. Dad called our church and left a message that, whichever pastor returned first, we would baptize you at 11 a.m. If a pastor was available, then we'd like to have him there. No one came. We closed the door, baptized you, and prayed, and then dad had to go back to work. By the time the technologist was ready to do your bone scan, you were sleeping. She took a chance and went ahead without sedating you. I stood by your side as she moved sandbags around your body to keep you in place.

Halfway through the scan, I saw Pastor Ron sitting outside the door, praying. His eye caught mine. He came in and stayed with us through the remainder of the scan. You slept on. Daddy came back, and we moved to another area. No, we wouldn't be allowed to go with you for the CT scan, so the three of us prayed while you continued to sleep, unaided, through this final test.

Now Jessica Leigh, newly baptized child of God, it is only hours since your Baptism and tests were completed. Your bruise is already visibly fading. The doctors say there is no sign of a tumor and no indication as to what caused the bruise. You are a healthy child.

Now we can get back to doing what other new parents do—listening to advice, playing with the new baby, and going for walks. We'll compare you to the baby growth and development charts; try to get the house in order, meals cooked, and thank-you notes written; and handle the day-to-day stress and strain of too little sleep and too much to do.

"Well, you're done nursing, and I guess it's time to say good night. I love you. Daddy loves you, and Jesus loves you, Jessica. May the Lord bless you and keep you. May the Lord make His face shine on you and be gracious to you. The Lord lift up His countenance upon you and give you peace and a good night's sleep. In the name of the Father and of the Son and of the Holy Spirit. Amen. See you in two hours, Jess."

"Kim, Jessica's crying, wake up!"

"Don't worry, Bruce, she's right here. I'm holding her. Wait, where is she?"

"You really must be tired, Kim; Jess is in her crib, and you're in our bed. I'll get her."

It's a good thing it's Saturday and Bruce is home. My thoughts won't focus. I don't think I can make it through another day. Maybe I can get some sleep and a shower before I have to meet Cathy (alias today's perfect corporate executive and mother) and Diane ("I lost all but five pounds when Andrea was born") for lunch. A once-a-month mom's luncheon at Emily's restaurant sure sounded great when our husbands suggested it while we were all pregnant. Now I'm not so sure. I can't even keep track of where my child is—I'll probably fall asleep in my soup. Besides, they're both back at their stimulating, professional careers, and I'm just a sleepy mom.

What can I possibly add to the conversation? Changing diapers, breast-feeding on demand, cooking, cleaning, and rocking my baby aren't exactly the topics boardroom decisions are based on. Can our friendships survive our changing life-styles? Can I survive lunch? Can I even get into my pre-maternity jeans?

Maybe if I lie on the bed and flatten my stomach I'll be able to pull the (umph) zipper (ugh) up—I got it. The first major triumph—getting back into my old clothes. Now all I have to do is move, eat, and breathe without splitting a seam.

"So, how's the newest mom on the block?" Cathy began after we ordered our first cup of tea and the soup-and-sandwich special of the day. The aroma of fresh baked breads, homemade food, and a variety of fresh ground coffees and herbal teas always helped put life back into a more relaxed perspective. "I can't imagine what you went through. Eight hours of labor was enough for me" she continued.

"Yeah, you had it easy, Cathy. Remember I had 24 hours of labor and didn't dilate so Andrea was born by C-section. But that had its benefits too. Mark wasn't sure about handling a baby. He had never been around them much. But when she was born and I was still under the anesthetic, he got to give Andrea her first bottle. He's really been cute to watch—he's such a proud papa," Diane commented.

"Bruce has been a real help too. He was a great coach in the birthing room, but 21 hours of labor was enough," I added. "I've decided the final outcome is what matters, though. I wouldn't trade Jessica for anything. I'm just glad she's healthy."

"That's how I feel now too," Diane added, sipping her blackberry tea. "We couldn't figure out what we were doing wrong those first couple of days when the baby was so cranky. Then my mother-in-law said Andrea had symptoms of thrush. She was right. The medicine's helped, but now that my mother-in-law was right, I'm sure I'll be receiving even more advice from her. We want her to be involved with her grandchild, but she needs to accept the fact that we're Andrea's parents and we're going to raise our baby the way we believe is best. Then there was my mom who came over to help. I told her Andrea had to stay awake for a while so she'd nurse and sleep later. Mom rocked her to sleep instead. I wasn't real pleased," she added sarcastically.

"We went through some of that too," Cathy jumped in. "Everyone seems to have their story to tell and advice to share. And *everyone* wants to hold the baby. Why, at church I still have to hunt for him so we can go home, Josh gets passed around so much."

"Well, we've been a little more protective of Jess with her being on the monitor. She doesn't get passed around so much. But you know, we really have appreciated our friends and the people at church. The prayer support and concern has been wonderful. And the meals people brought were tremendous. Maybe that's why I'm not losing this weight. I'm afraid Bruce got spoiled though—we got used to a hot dinner being delivered at 5 p.m. Now that I'm cooking, dinner's not always ready when he gets home. Oh well, we'll just adjust. Besides, depending on what the baby's doing, sometimes

Bruce eats while I care for Jess and then I eat. Speaking of food, here's ours."

After bowing our heads for silent prayer, Cathy picked the conversation right up again. "I wish people had helped us that way. Fortunately, I had frozen a few casseroles before Josh was born, and our mothers helped us out too. We had lots of cards and phone calls, though. Sometimes I wished I could have signaled people some way so they wouldn't call when I was trying to sleep. I finally gave in and turned on the answering machine and returned calls later."

"And when you're home during the day you get so many sales calls and door-to-door sales people or surveys, it's sometimes hard to get anything done. I finally put up a sign by our front door that said 'Child sleeping, please knock,' so that at least Andrea could sleep," Diane continued. "People seem to appreciate being warned. Did you find a pediatrician for Jessica? I didn't have one picked out, and because of insurance, I could only select one from a certain medical group. We have narrowed our choices down to two doctors just by talking to other parents—there were 14 births among those in my office alone in the past year, so I had plenty of referrals. But with the C-section, I got to stay in the hospital longer and know the doctors better. As it turned out, I liked one and couldn't stand the other one. So I chose the one I liked. When I asked him 'What happens if I want you for Andrea's doctor?' you could see the glow in his face. He's so personable; we feel real comfortable with his judgments and talking with him."

"Well," I jumped in, "we interviewed a doctor who had been recommended. We liked him and decided he'd be the one to treat Jessica. After all she's been through, I'm sure we made the right choice. You know what I mean, Diane; Andrea was sick and colicky."

"I know. Most of the time we really enjoyed her, but I remember one day I was so tired and sick of hearing her cry that I called a friend and offered to sell Andrea real cheap. My friend has two young children and had just been told the oldest has cerebral palsy. Then I felt really bad because Andrea was only crying. My friend had so much more to cope with than me, and I was the one complaining. She's got such a good attitude and says she can already see God's hand in how their lives are developing."

"Are you sure you're going to stay home and be a full-time mom?" Cathy asked. "You were so involved in your department and in volunteer and professional organizations too." (Somehow I knew this question would be raised today.) I'd drive myself and Joshua crazy if I made that decision," she continued. "This way we spend quality time together; I use my education, and we can still afford our before-baby lifestyle. I only felt a little guilty putting Josh in day care at first, but then I saw how much he likes being around so many others and the guilt passed. As long as I don't have to stay at the office too late, it works out fine. Oh, don't get me wrong; I miss him and look forward to picking him up at the end of the day. Then I either stop for carry-out food or quickly heat up one of the casseroles I made over the weekend. I don't know what people did before microwaves. We get tired of fast food sometimes, but it gives us a chance to spend more time together as a family instead of working so long in the kitchen. Fortunately, Josh hasn't been sick a lot. We still haven't had to tackle the question of who will stay home first or most often when Josh does get sick. Really, Kim, don't you think you'll miss the challenge and mental stimulation of your professional career in marketing?"

"Why should she?" Diane piped in. "I, for one, am envious. I hate leaving Andrea with a sitter, even for the few hours before Mark gets home and after I leave for work. But what choice do I have? After all, his job is temporary. With the current economic situation, none of the companies want to hire another full-time person in his field. So instead he bounces back and forth between the company that laid him off and a few others. That way they don't have the personnel expense. God willing, he'll find permanent employment soon. But for now, I'm the one who has the health insurance and we need that. I hope that someday we'll reach the point where we can live comfortably on one or one-and-a-half salaries and then I can be home while Andrea grows up. I already feel like I'm missing out on so much when I'm away from her. I don't want a sitter to see her take her first step or say her first word."

"Fortunately, I've got a small, family-oriented child care center where the caregiver is willing to take photos and keep a brief diary of Josh's day so I can tell exactly what happened each day—if he napped well, was happy, and whatever else went on," Cathy added. "It's one way I can keep in touch with his everyday life, and it gives me a good indication of what temperament I'll be dealing with through the night. In some ways, I think having a happy, working mom will help Josh understand that God gave us each talents to use whether as a computer programmer, banker, full-time mother, or whatever. But enough; we've been monopolizing the conversation. Kim, how are you really doing?"

"I'm fine when I'm actually awake. A long shower really helped today."

"Oh, Jess will start sleeping longer soon, and you'll feel more human then. I remember I was so glad when the first three months and the colic were over! I'd get so frustrated that I'd get Mark to put Andrea in the car and drive her around so she would sleep. That way I got some peace and time to refresh my nerves," Diane said.

"My quiet time comes when I put Jessica to bed at night and during late-night feedings. We've got a Bible and a booklight set out on the table next to the rocking chair in Jess' room. I can read and stay awake while she nurses. But one gift I really appreciate is a tape of John Michael Talbot's music 'Evening' and 'Morning.' We turn on the tape at bedtime. It's soothing for both Jess and me. And it helps refocus my thoughts from the day so they're centered on God."

"Aren't you concerned that she's getting enough food? With a bottle you can at least tell how much a baby eats; you can share those late-night feedings, and it's *so* much more convenient," Cathy responded.

"Yes, amount of food was a concern at first, but my mom gave us a baby scale, and we weighed Jessica before and after feedings a few times to be sure she was eating plenty for someone her age and size. As for bottles, Bruce gets to give Jess a bottle of either breast milk or formula about once a day. Jessica also gets bottle-fed when we're out somewhere where I don't feel comfortable nursing and when I'm too tired to get out of bed one more time. She's only slept through the night once so far."

"I think you're avoiding my question about returning to work," Cathy prodded.

"One thing I had hoped to avoid today is jeopardizing our friendships by getting into what they're calling 'mommy wars' between those who return to careers and those who choose to stay home with their children. But I really have no regrets. Fortunately, Bruce and I had talked about having children while we were doing all of our premarital planning. We decided all of our bills would always be based on Bruce's income so I'd be able to stay home with our children. I'm sure that'll mean we'll have fewer 'things,' and maybe we won't live in our dream house. The house we do have though is a home filled with love. And I'll always be available for both Bruce's needs and those of our children."

"But not all of us have a choice," Diane stated.

I took a deep breath and went on. "I know not everyone has a choice, but I have a hard time understanding how a mother can leave her infant with strangers and not feel guilty. Now that Jessica's health problems are resolved, she and I are having so much fun together. Since she's with me, I'm sure her day will be spent in a Christian environment. Bruce only works seven minutes from home and joins us every day for lunch. Jess is a great traveler. She has already frequented a few of the area's top restaurants, sat through our weekly small-group Bible study, and even attended a friend's wedding. And it's so exciting to witness each new accomplishment. I really consider it a privilege, first, to have been used by God to give Jessica life, and second, to be able to be home with her to nurture her—to be a full-time wife and mother."

"Tell us some more about 'mommy wars,' " Cathy interrupted.

"You know, the reading I've done on 'mommy wars' talks about the stay-at-home mom as someone who can't put her finger on what she's accomplished in any given day. I already know that feeling.

"She has peace of mind because she's been there with her child through play time, all of the 'firsts,' and all of the comical and serious events in her child's life. But she feels left out or excluded from conversations with other adults as if being a full-time mother reduces her to a mindless individual. Sometimes I'm finding myself more concerned with things like diaper rash and toilet training than many current events, such as war in the Middle East or hunger in Africa.

"Stay-at-home moms accept the monetary trade-offs and lack of personal time. Since many of them have come out of the corporate world, they understand that the stress of motherhood feels equivalent to giving a presentation at work all day.

"A stay-at-home mom feels secure in her decision to stay at home and feels sorry for those who consider her 'trapped' in motherhood. And she sees the extraordinary in the ordinary occurrences of everyday life."

"On the other hand," Cathy jumped in, "as a 'working' mom who really wants to be in the work force, I'm committed to having an active, successful professional life *and* being a great parent."

"Working moms have to accept the price of going to work—the guilt we feel following our child's comments or requests like 'Can't you stay home and play with me today, Mommy?' " Diane continued.

"Sometimes I think I'd go crazy if I weren't working," Cathy added. "But working moms must find ways to deal with child care, sickness, meals, and pressure from co-workers. Sometimes we even look at work as an escape from the stress of caring for a colicky or difficult baby."

"I know I'll hear offensive, disheartening, and upsetting remarks from neighbors, friends, my pastor, and others close to me. But I think about my baby in between appointments, work schedules, and other activities and give up my free time at home to spend with Andrea," Diane said.

"I think both groups feel looked down on and both want the best of everything for their children. We all believe what we are doing is best for our children, for our families, and for ourselves," Cathy commented.

"So why, when moms get together, does the type of work a mom does automatically create tension?" I shot back. "Can't we just go on accepting each other as the individual, special creations of God that we liked before we had babies and continue to do things together?

"I'm sorry. I guess my feelings were stronger than I realized, and I just needed to get it all out in the open."

"I'm glad you did," Cathy quietly replied. "The 'mommy wars' you talked about really do exist—sometimes in very subtle but hurtful ways. The last time I went to the evening women's group at church all of the moms who stay at home sat and talked together. I could tell they didn't approve of my baby being in a child care situation. So, yes, the three of us can go on with our friendship …"

"Only now we have even more to talk about—like being the best moms God created us to be," Diane enthusiastically interjected. "So what's our next adventure?"

"Well, you were right, Bruce. We ate too much and topped off lunch with Emily's luscious turtle cheesecake, talked about babies, child development, baby-sitters, and crafts. Oh, by the way, we've already set the date of our next lunch together, only this time we're going to the craft fair at the college and then to lunch.

"Cathy, Diane, and I haven't really changed—just our perspectives have been altered a little. We're all concerned about the same things—priorities, time management, and being good, Christian wives and mothers. Our friendships are going to survive motherhood too.

"As I was getting back into the car, Diane had the audacity to say, 'Hang in there, Kim, it does get better. Maybe by the time they're teenagers we'll all get the sleep we think we need.' And all I could respond was 'Not a chance, Diane. Then we'll be worrying about why they're out late.'"

"Sounds like you three had a good time. I'm glad you went. It's good to see you joking and smiling," Bruce said.

"I'm glad I went too. For now, though, I've simply got to get out of these jeans!"

"Lord, make me an instrument of Your peace ..." the John Michael Talbot tape begins.

"Well, Jessica, we've gone through a lot together these first few months. The monitor wires breaking, health concerns ... but even your DPT shot and polio vaccine didn't seem to bother you much. You took it all calmly and helped us with your frequent smiles.

"Last night's pneumogram while you slept showed your longest apnea spell at 11 seconds. Irregular breathing was .04 percent of the time. You're considered normal. We can take you off the monitor whenever we're ready. Those were Dr. Schmidt's orders today, Jess. Dad and I think we'll be ready by morning. We'll thank God and ask Him to continue to be in control of your life and health.

"What timing—Dad wants us to travel with him in two weeks. I guess I'd better start thinking about how many diapers we'll need for the trip and working out the logistics. It's surprising how many others I've met since you were born who brought their babies home on monitors. Everyone's scared and yet joyfully anticipates this night—the last with the monitor. I had no idea how frightened I'd be to take it off. But you are God's child, Jessica. Now let's see. Tonight I get to read and meditate on Psalm 103.

> Praise the LORD, O my soul;
> all my inmost being, praise his holy name.
> Praise the LORD, O my soul,

> and forget not all his benefits—
> who forgives all your sins
>   and heals all your diseases,
> who redeems your life from the pit
>   and crowns you with love and compassion,
> who satisfies your desires with good things
>   so that your youth is renewed like the eagle's. ...
>
> The LORD is compassionate and gracious,
>   slow to anger, abounding in love. ...
> For as high as the heavens are above the earth,
>   so great is his love for those who fear him;
> as far as the east is from the west,
>   so far has he removed our transgressions from us.
> As a father has compassion on his children,
>   so the LORD has compassion on those who fear
>   him. ...
> But from everlasting to everlasting
>   the LORD's love is with those who fear him,
>   and his righteousness with their children's
>   children. ...
> Praise the LORD, O my soul.
>
> (Ps. 103:1–5, 8, 11–13, 17, 22 NIV).

Yes, Lord, Your mercy is everlasting. You constantly forgive our sins. You heal us of every disease—even worry, fatigue, and apnea. You redeemed me. You satisfy my desires with good things. You restore my strength and help me survive those sleepless nights. Your compassion and love overwhelm me. You are indeed my loving, caring, compassionate, understanding, all-powerful Father now and forever. I praise You and thank You, O Lord.

Done Jess? May the Lord bless you and keep you. May the Lord make His face shine on you and be gracious to you. The Lord lift up His countenance upon you and give you peace and a good night's sleep. In the name of the Father and of the Son and of the Holy Spirit. Amen. There you go. Sleep well.

Yes, Lord, make me an instrument of Your peace—especially in the lives of Bruce and Jessica.

Thank You for this precious miracle You have given me in this child. She is indeed a glorious gift from You. Help me to love her as You love each of us and to enjoy each precious moment with her.

When I feel the anxiety, fear, and frustrations of being a parent, remind me that motherhood was Your idea, and not only do You understand everything about how Your invention works, but You stand with me, teach me, and counsel me as I help to raise this child in Your love. Help me to acquire the skills and apply the principles needed to be a good mother to Jessica. Guide my attitudes and emotions to be beneficial to her and pleasing to You.

Your love is perfect—more than shallow sentimentality. Help me to be involved in her life in a patient, kind, hopeful, cheerful, self-giving manner. Let Your Holy Spirit pour out Your love in my heart. Reveal Your true nature to me and help me to be a true woman of God.

Help our family to grow and mature and be all You intend us to be. Build our house upon Your faithful rock. Bless our marriage. Fulfill the needs of my family and myself. Guide, guard, equip, and protect us, Lord, that together we may serve You and Your people.

Help me to enjoy motherhood and to follow my baby's example and trust and love You completely just as she trusts and loves me. Let me keep an open mind and heart for what this child can teach me and live in anticipation of what joy each new moment may bring. Mold me, shape me, renew me, fill me so that I may be the mother and wife and person You created me to be. In the name of Jesus, my risen Lord, I pray.

Good night, Lord ... and thank You, again. Amen.

An Encouraging Word

From a distance, motherhood seems so simple, so natural. Two people fall in love, get married, conceive, and give birth. That child grows up, falls in love, gets married, conceives, and gives birth. The life cycle continues from generation to generation, through the centuries, reaching as far back as Adam and Eve.

> So God created man in his own image, in the image of God he created him; male and female he created them. God blessed them and said to them, "Be fruitful and increase in number; fill the earth and subdue it." (Gen. 1:27–28 NIV)

Motherhood, so elusive to those who hope and wait, and so binding for all who have joined the association. Entry into this exclusive group called mothers is not always the same or as easy as a quick glance at history would lead a woman to believe.

Conception

"I'm pregnant." It is not difficult to visualize a series of women saying these same two little words but using them to express very different emotions.

"I'm pregnant—how am I going to tell my family and friends. I'm single, unmarried, and didn't plan to join this sorority of motherhood so soon."

"I'm pregnant, and I'm scared. This is my third child. The doctor advised me not to get pregnant again. He felt my health and even life could be in danger because of my diabetes and other complications."

"I'm pregnant and I don't want to be. My children are

finally grown, and I am just finally beginning my own career, my own life."

"The E.P.T. test is positive. I'm pregnant. My husband and I are so happy. We can't wait to tell our parents and friends the joyful news. Everything is working out right. God is so good to us. This is perfect timing."

"It worked. I can't believe it. I'm pregnant. We have been trying for so long. I'd almost given up. The infertility specialist knew what he was talking about. I'm pregnant. I'M PREGNANT. I'M PREGNANT. Rah! Yea, Dr. Adamson!"

Pregnancy

Pregnancy is the beginning of a special creative connection with a woman's own personal genealogical line and with all women throughout history. It is her connection with God's plan for humanity. God has given woman a very distinctive role in creation, the ability to provide a safe place in her uterus for a new creation of God to develop. Our heavenly Father's creative hand is active in the development of each and every embryo.

> Before I formed you in the womb I knew you.
> (Jer. 1:5 NIV)

> Blessed are you among women, and blessed is
> the child you will bear! (Luke 1:42 NIV)

Pregnancy is also the beginning of a very special bond between a mother and her child. This is an extraordinary time of life when a woman feels and knows a new life, a new creation, is growing inside of her. The new life is completely dependent on her, the mother, for physical nurture and emotional stability for these first 277 days of existence. This is a life that is a part of her, connected to her by that tiny life-giving umbilical cord. This is also a life that can be traced to her genetically through a DNA workup.

Ultrasound and TV screens monitoring the baby's movements put a slightly new twist on pregnancy and motherhood. The new generation baby books start with the baby's first ultrasound picture. Today the new mother can see as well as feel her new infant long before his or her actual birth day.

While nothing is mentioned in Kim's story about prenatal care, taking care of that tiny infant in utero becomes a high priority for most conscientious mothers. No alcohol. No cigarettes. No drugs, even prescribed ones, without the doctor's advice, especially during the first trimester. Eating nutritionally balanced meals, taking mega vitamins, and getting proper exercise take on new meaning when a mother is doing it for both herself and her infant. The unborn child is completely dependent on one person, and one person only, his or her mother.

Birth

The big day, the day of labor and delivery for mom, the birth day for the baby. The first moments of separation for both are critical. Both must be able to exist separately from one another without being physically attached.

The first few moments and hours after delivery seem awkward. The mother can begin to move around without her child. She can wear clothes again that don't look like a tent built for two. The baby leaves the warm, secure, climate-controlled environment inside his or her mother and finds a way to live and breath in the bright, somewhat abrasive, and oft-polluted atmosphere called earth.

After the birth, the mother basically determines the degree of dependence and symbiosis the two will have one with another for the first few months and years. There appears to be a great deal of flexibility and choice available to mothers in determining care for their infant. There are a wide range of acceptable options. The degree of closeness will be determined by the amount of time the mother spends with the infant and how she chooses to spend the time with the infant.

There is a continuum of degree of closeness that could

become unhealthy for both mother and child if carried to either extreme. The mother who is too close, who smothers her child, who will not allow the child to develop independently of her may find a child that has trouble functioning in the world later. On the other hand, the mother who disengages from her child even though she is feeding and providing food for her child may find an infant that is not surviving. A baby that is not emotionally nurtured will loose weight and develop marasmus. This is a condition of progressive emancipation in infants that occurs when an emotional bond is not formed between the infant and the mother. The infant may have to be moved to another caretaker who is able to connect with the child on an emotional basis or the infant will die.

This is not a problem for Kim and Jessica. Kim's protective and motherly instincts are certainly evident after her baby is born. She knows there is a problem with her baby before the doctor even talks to her. She senses how the baby feels and keeps up a constant chatter with Jess as the child goes through test after test. Only a mother, or a person with strong motherly instincts, would desire to continue such a steady stream of consciousness directed at her infant.

Kim chooses to have a great deal of closeness with Jess. She quits her job, breast-feeds Jess, and devotes herself to Jess' care. Her thoughts and her energy are primarily devoted to Jess.

Other women today may choose, or feel forced out of economic necessity, to continue their careers during their child's early years. Each woman is unique. God did not bless all women with the same abilities and talents. Some women have a capacity, in fact a drive, to be very involved in any number of projects, whether they are doing volunteer activity or working in a paid position. Other women have the ability to focus on the detail work of their home and family, making their home a restorative haven and refuge for all who stop by. Women are different in many ways, but they are almost universally alike in wanting to establish a positive connection with their child and to be thought of by all as a "good mother."

All Is Not Perfect

What happens to a mother when she first discovers her child has a problem, her child is not perfect, her child may not survive. When we fail in our quest to be gods ourselves, we still hope our children will somehow be perfect, angelic, and godlike. Sooner or later all women, like Kim, discover children are flawed by original sin and the fallen nature of humankind. Sooner or later, all mothers realize the imperfection in that angelic-looking infant or toddler.

A child who has a breathing problem and is hooked up to an apnea monitor is obviously not normal and often is more than a woman bargains for. No new mother sits around during pregnancy visualizing her child on an apnea monitor after birth. No new mother is thrilled at the prospect of having to use CPR to keep her child alive. In addition to those stresses, Kim and Bruce had an added burden when they were told that Jessica might have a tumor. To make a rational decision to allow Jessica to undergo life-threatening tests is difficult. To baptize one's own child and put her in God's hands takes courage and faith and trust.

Under similar circumstances, many mothers would look back and question whether they had done something that caused their baby to have a problem. They might ask: Why did the baby come early? Was I doing too much? Was I too active? Did I skip the vitamin pills a few too many days or not eat right? The close bond mothers and infants have, the sense of complete responsibility, and the belief that bad things only happen to bad people, may make women question if God is punishing them. Why did God allow their baby to have imperfections? Maybe they are being punished for something they did wrong. Perhaps they were indiscriminate about their sexuality in times past. Perhaps they nag at their husbands more than they should. Perhaps they don't read the Holy Scriptures enough or worship from the heart. If only ... if only ... if only they had done something differently perhaps the child would have been healthy.

Bargaining, making a deal with God, is a typical Christian

mother's response. "If you let my baby live, I will be more faithful, help fold bulletins every week, or dedicate my infant's life to you as Hanna of old did with Samuel." There finally comes a time when each Christian woman realizes she needs to trust solely in God's grace and forgiveness and place her infant in God's loving gracious hands. God's protective care surrounds both mother and child. He will be with them through the crisis of the day, month, year, or even a lifetime. Kim and Bruce called on this God of grace through water and Word "in the name of the Father and of the Son and of the Holy Spirit" and entrusted Jess to their heavenly Father.

Kim and Bruce were blessed. Their child was healed. The problem was serious but not ongoing and chronic. The bruise on Jess' face faded. Jess did not have a tumor. Many mothers have to face prominent defects in their children such as Down's syndrome, other forms of mental retardation, cerebral palsy, or other serious deformities of body or mind. To have a child of sound body and sound mind is a blessing. But in our fallen world, a low but certain percentage of all infants born will have major defects. Some impairments are predictable because the mother is an alcoholic or is addicted to a drug. Sometimes mental retardation or Huntington's Chorea runs in the family. Sometimes there is absolutely no explanation for why an infant was born with a significant chromosome imbalance and is not expected to live.

Some infants die. God in His infinite wisdom will not give us more than we can bear, but there is a definite difference in the burdens we are asked to carry.

The prospect of a new baby, a bright-eyed, adorable child, brings new life and hope into almost any family. That childlike hope and trust and genuine enjoyment of little dolls or chocolate chip cookies is such a welcome relief to adults who have become burdened down and disillusioned with the disappointments and drudgeries of everyday living. To breastfeed your child or have your little one grab your hand gives you a feeling that there is someone who still believes and trusts in you, who believes you are okay, and who gives you significance in this hustling, bustling, highly populated, computerized world.

Having a child or infant who dies brings unbelievable pain and suffering to the new parents, especially the mother, who has already established an intimate iron-clad bond. Defects and the death of babies, these new, perfect-looking creations, are unnatural. The quick contrast of emotional experience is unique.

To go from the height of joy in being a part of the creative process of birth to the depth of despair is a devastating and disastrous fall. This fall can send women into a depression that lasts a lifetime. These same women, with support from family and friends and a firm faith in God's providential care, can move on with their lives. They can learn to trust and live again. They can reach an equilibrium and return to a level of functioning equal to or higher than before the trauma with their child occurred.

A woman gives birth and joins the creative chain of creation, but at some point she realizes this child will grow and prosper without her. The mother exists separate from her child. She is a person in her own right. She must find her own joy. She must not only live through the laughter in her child's eyes. She must be aware of her own needs and find laughter in her own eyes. She dare not sublimate and sacrifice for her child in a manner that would deny her own needs and endanger the joy of the mother-child relationship.

A challenge for new mothers involves living in the world of their newborn as well as living in and being a part of the larger world. Kim and her friends were aware of their needs for female bonding as they met for lunch and set the date for their next get-together. Adult women have needs for adult companionship, both male and female. They have a need to run and play with other adults. They have a need to stimulate their minds on an adult level, to read, to create. Lunch with the girls, a date with her husband, a class in ceramics or computer engineering can keep the creative process alive within a woman. This is not only important for the new mother but also for the infant. Later on, the child will need a positive role model as he or she enters the world and begins to leave his or her own creative mark.

Predictions

What can we predict for the future for Kim and her family? What patterns of behavior are demonstrated in her story? Kim is a person who faces problems, makes decisions, and takes action all in the name of our Lord and Savior.

Kim shared many of the problems she faced in her account of the experience of being a new mother. She had problems conceiving and carrying a child. She went into premature labor without her own doctor. She also had to face Jessica's breathing problem, Jessica's diarrhea, the bruise on her face, the life-threatening testing procedures, the possibility of vanishing relationships with her friends, and the expired license plates.

Kim is aware of these problems and issues. She has willingly and openly shared her thoughts and feelings with Bruce, with her friends, and even with Jessica, who cannot yet understand.

In addition, Kim takes action. She went to an infertility specialist, learned how to use an apnea monitor, and learned how to administer CPR. She contacted the doctor about the ongoing diarrhea and the growing bruise on Jessica's face. She took Jessica to the hospital for tests and made the decision with Bruce about the emergency Baptism. She addressed the subject of "mommy wars" with her friends.

Kim will probably function quite well throughout her life. She is able to assess the situation. She has the ability to be aware of problem situations. She does not panic. She uses good judgment, makes wise decisions, and then takes action. She uses music, Scripture, and conversation to calm herself and to organize her thoughts. Her follow-through is excellent, even when she is tired or plagued by postpartum hormonal imbalances.

One cannot predict what circumstances Kim will

encounter as Jessica grows up, but it is evident that Kim has the tools to survive and move forward with a positive, steady force.

She will have her place in the genealogical history of the world. She, like so many women though the ages, now has a place in the life cycle of God's world.

Shirley Schaper

Reflection

- Before you became pregnant, how did you picture motherhood? During pregnancy how did your picture change? How does the daily reality of caring for an infant compare to your earlier dreams and expectations?
- What effect has motherhood had on your relationship with your husband? Are you closer? more distant? How do you account for these changes?
- Who has been most supportive of you as you begin your new role as "mother"?
- Have you noticed changes in friendships? If so, how have these relationships changed?
- Why is it important, especially when you feel frustrated, tired, isolated, or when you feel like running away, to reaffirm your relationship with God? How does God encourage you to see yourself in Is. 43:1; Ps. 100:3; Rom. 5:8; 8:15–17; 1 Cor. 3:16; and 1 John 3:1?
- What encouragement do you hear God speaking to you in Ps. 55:22; 145:18; Prov. 3:6; Rom. 8:38–39; 2 Cor. 1:3–4; and 1 Peter 5:7?
- How can you and other women best serve new mothers in your congregation or community?
- How will you respond to stay-at-home moms? To "working" moms? How can you be an instrument of peace and encouragement for them?
- Does your congregation offer support for parents facing difficult health situations with their infants? Any form of ongoing assistance?

If you identify with these two familiar cries of new mothers—"I can't get everything done!" and "I'm losing myself!"—then try one or more of the following:

- Talk with friends on a regular basis, especially those who are relatively new mothers. Just as handicrafters like to compare projects with others who have similar interests, new mothers need that sharing too.
- Get plenty of rest—even if it means hiring a baby-sitter or placing a sign on the door saying, "Mother and baby are sleeping—please write a message on the pad of paper provided" or turning on an answering machine.
- Be flexible—housework will keep or can be done by willing friends or relatives.
- Maintain or establish a devotion/prayer time. Continually ask God for help as a wife and mother. You can even read Scripture aloud to your baby. She's never too young to hear the Word and see your example.
- Create a "to do" list. Use it only as a guide and cross off anything completed.
- Establish your priorities—God, your baby/family, and you should have top priority. Everything else can be accomplished by someone else. Follow your doctor's recommendations for rest, exercise, and any health concerns. Don't blame yourself for emotional turmoil—seek assistance.
- Being a mother takes time and can be lots of fun. Enjoy the time you have to spend with your child, especially the time you have just to hold him or her.
- Subscribe to a publication such as *Christian Parenting Magazine*.
- Ask yourself, "What special things is God teaching me?"
- Allow yourself time without your child. Honestly express your feelings, needs, concerns, and joys with your spouse.
- Everyone likes to give advice to new parents. When someone approaches you, simply smile and be courteous. Listen to each person's advice. Then do what you believe is best for you and your child.

Dear Father,

You have worked Your miracle
in me.

I hold proof of Your great love
in my arms.

I thank You with all my heart
for this child.

What joy,
what comfort,
what strength
I find
in remembering when I am exhausted or fearful,
when I feel ill-equipped or inept,
that *You* are *my* Father
and that *You* hold *me,*
cherish me,
feed me,
protect me too.

You have high hopes for us, Father,
for this child and me.

Guide us and forgive us
and fill us with Yourself
that the life You so graciously give
will be lived
for You.

Amen.

Story 3

Connie: A Path Unplanned

by Kathleen Winkler

Connie

It's nearing midnight as I sit in this shadowy hospital waiting room. Jenny's somewhere behind closed doors, having her baby—while I wait here to pace and pray. The pop machine glows in the dimness and clunks softly. The coffee in the ever-perking pot simmers and thickens. I wait.

Carl is here with me, waiting for our baby to have her baby. So is Tony. A year ago, when Tony was caught in the whirl of a life-style that I don't even want to think about, I never would have believed that he'd be sitting here beside me. But his little sister is important to him, important enough that the strains of their relationship (and ours, for that matter) are forgotten in the tension of waiting for this new life. I wish Jenny's two sisters could be here too, but they're off at college—exams won't wait.

It's hard to stay awake. I slump in the orange plastic chair and try to doze. My head propped uncomfortably against the hard wall, I drift and dream.

Twenty years. Where did they go? My thoughts flow back, almost against my will. I don't really want to think about all we've come through, but somehow I have to, maybe God wants me to. Maybe He's saying, "See what I've brought you through? See where you are today?"

That new baby working so hard to be born represents more than just another generation. He or she, and the fact that we are all here waiting, represents a triumph. A triumph of a family's love over huge odds, over enormous conflict. We're very different people from what I imagined 20 years ago. We *are* here. In some ways, that's a miracle as much as the new life.

I remember the days when I was a young girl. I was raised in the Lutheran church, baptized, went to Sunday school, and did all the things I thought were right—the things the church says are right and you are supposed to do.
I remember our wedding day. I floated down the aisle in white lace, carrying pale orchids. Carl was waiting for me, so handsome in his tux, strong and ready to take care of me. My dream was to have a wonderful Christian home with wonderful Christian children. I thought it was as simple as that. It was almost a Cinderella thing—oh, you might have a few struggles along the way, but once you marry that knight in shining armor and have those little darling babies and go to church, you won't have any real problems in your family. Do everything the biblical way and everything will be just fine. Carl and I had really committed our lives to the Lord and intended to raise our children to be fine, upstanding Christians.

The adoption counselor's office was cheery with its nursery rhyme posters on the wall and a bank of photos of ecstatic new moms and dads holding the babies the agency had placed with them. I never thought Carl and I would be here. It was a blow when we found out that medical problems meant we'd never have a baby ourselves.
But even that blow was temporary—adoption was so easy back in the '60s. Abortion wasn't yet legal; there were lots of babies who needed families.
"I've got good news," the social worker said. "You passed your home study with flying colors. We know you'll make wonderful parents, and I'm pretty sure we'll have a baby for you very soon."
Carl and I went out to lunch to celebrate. We'd made it— we were officially stamped and approved: GOOD PARENTS.
The counselor was right. Within a couple of weeks the phone call came. "We've got a baby boy for you. He's so cute, with the most enormous eyes. He's seven months old, and you can pick him up next Tuesday."
Our lives changed forever, as they do for every new par-

ent. Tony became the center of our lives. It wasn't long before we wanted another baby; again it was easy to adopt, and Carrie joined our family. A couple of years later, Susan joined her sister and brother.

I surface again—my neck is screaming at me that it's in no position to sleep. Maybe a short stroll down to the drinking fountain will ease my cramped muscles. But even as I move soundlessly on my rubber-soled sneakers, past the dimly lit nurses' station, my thoughts return to the past.

I remember those hectic but rewarding years with what we thought was our complete, loving family.

A warm, breezy September morning floats into my mind. "You're going to just love kindergarten, honey," I reassured bravely as Susan clambered onto the big yellow bus. I trudged up the driveway and into the silent house. "Well, Mom, they're all gone now," I said into a cup of cold coffee. "You're almost 30. What are you going to do with the rest of your life?"

The sunlight still streamed into the social worker's office, the nursery rhyme posters still marched around the walls, only the bank of photos had changed. It was bigger.

"Well, Connie, I'm glad to see you again and hear about your family. I knew when we approved you that you and Carl would be good parents, and your kids sure seem fine. We'd love to have you as clients again, but I have to warn you. Things are different now. Very different."

The '70s—*Roe v. Wade* had turned the adoption picture upside down. Babies were scarce; eager couples were lined up six deep, clamoring for each available healthy infant.

"Since you already have three adopted kids, we can't really give you another one. Unless you'd be willing to take a child with a handicap."

I felt like a bomb had been dropped on me. "Let me have some time to think about this. Call me in a couple of weeks." I left in confusion.

When the social worker called back and described some

of the severely handicapped children they were trying to place, I wasn't sure I could manage them. I again asked for time to think.

One hot summer morning a few weeks later, the phone rang. "We have a four-month-old baby girl for placement right now. She was born with part of her stomach and intestine missing."

"How do you feed her?" I asked. The case worker explained that she had to be fed through a tube connected to the normal part of her system.

Once she reached a weight of 30 pounds, the surgeons felt her problems could be corrected and she would live a normal life.

In the meantime, she had just been released from the hospital to a foster home. The case worker assured me that she was easy to care for and the foster mother wasn't having any problems at all.

She kept talking, and while I had started out thinking I couldn't handle this, before I hung up the phone, I blurted, "I'll think about it."

The case worker sent me the application forms, but they sat in my kitchen drawer for weeks. I kept thinking, "I've got a nice life with three healthy children, why would I want to take this on?" But in the back of my mind, a thought kept nagging: That little girl needs a home, and we have a home to offer.

The social worker called back to ask why I hadn't sent in the forms. "I just can't make up my mind," I said. She thought the next step should be a visit to see the baby.

"She's a wonderful baby," her foster mother raved. "And you should see her beautiful smile." I looked at her and I could feel the tug at my heart. The social worker told me not to feel pressured, that there were other families willing to take her, but that we were her first choice.

I went home and prayed about it. I do think that God answers prayers, but I don't know anyone who has had an angel appear at her bedside and say, "This is what you should do." And I certainly didn't receive such a visit. But slowly the certainty grew that this felt right and it was the right thing for us. I felt that if God let us have that baby, He would give me the strength to take care of her. So I said yes.

As I walk back to the waiting room my mind flashes back to those early months with Jenny, to the stomachaches, diarrhea, and digestion problems. I could see her in my mind, such a pretty baby with a lovely smile. But she was so insecure, a mommy's baby. Long after other babies will go to other people, she would cry and cling when approached by anyone other than family.

Everything we did for her seemed to take three times as long as we thought it would. Her feeding tube got infected several times. It could take hours to get her to sleep, rocking and soothing her. She didn't sleep through the night until she was three. There were times when I'd wake up hearing her cry and think, I can't get up one more time. But somehow I did what I had to do.

And realistically, part of the problem was me. I was such a perfectionist that it never occurred to me that I could say, "Someone else will have to make Thanksgiving dinner this year because I can't manage this baby and make a four-course dinner for 35." If the PTA needed 50 cupcakes, I never said, "I can't do that." I baked the 50 cupcakes.

It was probably a good thing I didn't know how hard it was going to be. If I had known, I might have said no to adopting her, and we would have missed having Jenny—and she's brought us so much joy. We would have missed a lot of pain, too, but you have to say that about all your kids, as well as anybody else you love. It's like C. S. Lewis said, "Love makes you vulnerable." And, of course, once we had her, she was ours and we loved her.

I settle back into the uncomfortable chair. It's torture to sit here.

I'd like to turn off my mind. I don't want to think about the years that came later when the older kids headed into high school. Tony shifts in his chair; his face, in sleep, loses its strain. I look at him in the soft lamplight, his eyelashes brushing his cheeks. He's so perfect, so classically good looking. I remember ...

On a sticky summer night the year between his junior and senior years in high school, faint lightening flickered on the horizon, thunder muttered softly in the distance. Maybe the crushing heat would end tonight in a rush of rain. I sat in the family room with Carl and the girls, trying to concentrate on the mindless TV program, but the churning in my own mind wouldn't let me.

Things hadn't been going well with Tony. He seemed to be having a hard time with what the world would call "finding himself." It started when he felt rejected in a sports-oriented, competitive, suburban culture because he didn't like sports and wasn't very good at them. "You're so smart and so musically talented and so good looking, and we love you just as you are," we assured him over and over. But it never seemed to sink in.

We tried to encourage him in music and gave him voice lessons but nothing seemed to help; he just became more unhappy, rebellious, and unpleasant to us. He came and went as he pleased, never telling us where he was going. He never shared anything with us, he didn't seem to have any friends—just acquaintances. Nobody ever called, nobody stayed for supper.

Our friends kept saying, "Don't worry, this is just what some boys go through." But somehow I felt that our children should have been immune to all that because we did what it says in Ephesians: "Raise your children in the nurture and admonition of the Lord." We sent them to Lutheran schools, took them to Sunday school and church, read *Little Visits with God* to them. We really felt we shouldn't have any problems.

We read all the books on dealing with adolescents we could get our hands on, tried seeing counselors at the high school and even our pastor. The pastor told us, "Don't worry about him. It's just adolescence, and it'll all come out in the wash." I didn't know what that meant—was I supposed to put Tony in the washing machine?

Other friends said, "Don't worry, all teenagers rebel, but they all get past it. He'll be fine." And some looked at us as if to say, "I'm not having problems with my children. I don't know what you've done wrong." I didn't need that—it just heaped on more guilt.

I had a gut feeling that it was more than teenage rebellion—that something was really wrong.

Just the night before, I had finally told Carl, "You always have that typical male attitude, 'Boys will be boys. Just let him go, and he'll turn out fine.' Well, things aren't going to turn out fine: There's something very wrong."

Carl had finally agreed that we had to confront Tony, to sit him down and say, "We know there's something terribly wrong, and we want to know what it is."

It was July 22, 1981—I'll never forget that date. Tony came in as the thunder began to build and said nothing as he headed through the family room toward the stairs.

"Tony, stop," I called after him. "We just can't go on like this anymore. We have to get to the bottom of what's wrong," I said.

He stopped on the stairs, turned back toward us. "Okay, I guess it's time you knew. But send Susan and Carrie upstairs."

With that I knew that it was something serious. I don't know if it was God protecting me from what I was about to hear, but I remember in those few seconds knowing that it was going to be the worst thing I'd ever heard in my life. But I knew that God was going to get me through it.

Tony sat tensely on the edge of the couch. "Mom, Dad, it's hard to tell you this, but I'm gay."

I felt as if my world had fallen apart. This can't be happening to us, I thought. This sort of thing doesn't happen to Christians. This doesn't happen to decent people. This only happens to people who never go to church or who have broken homes.

I stumbled up to bed that night with agony like acid pouring through my soul. I tossed and turned on my carefully selected, yellow flowered sheets. Suddenly things that had seemed so important—our home, the life I was trying to build for us—seemed like a mockery. I didn't know how I would ever live through this pain.

But at the same time, I was sure God would get us out of it. In my naivete, I really thought that we could just get Tony "fixed." We were Christians, after all, and the Bible has answers for everything, so all we had to do was take Tony to a counselor and he would change.

In the next few months, I read everything in the Bible I could find about homosexuality—and it was very evident that in God's eyes it is a sin. I also read everything else I could about the psychological aspects of homosexuality. There were so many divergent opinions: It's genetic. It's learned behavior. It's caused by family stress. The family has nothing to do with it. I found out even the experts are in the kindergarten stages of understanding homosexuality.

I looked back as much as I could on Tony's background. We don't know much about his birth parents—nothing about his father and little about his mother except that she was only 15, from a small town in rural Missouri, and her father was from the old country. Imagine being pregnant out of wedlock in a German Lutheran community in a small town in 1963. Could that have had any effect? I don't know.

The foster parents Tony lived with seemed like a wonderful, Christian family. Yet years later, a counselor told Tony that he showed the symptoms of sexual abuse as an infant. He has no conscious memory of anything like that happening to him. I suppose we will never know.

When I look back on it, I wonder how I ever got through those days. But somehow I did. Part of it was that I was so sure that God was going to rescue Tony. And part of it was just that I had so many people depending on me that I couldn't fall apart. Besides my own family, I was doing child care in my home—I had little babies dropped on my doorstep every morning who needed care. I had my girls: Susan was 15, Carrie 14, Jenny 10, and they needed me. I wanted to have a nervous breakdown. I wanted to just go away and pull the covers over my head and wake up when it was all gone, but I couldn't do that. I had to put one foot in front of another even though I had this horrible thing always in the back of my mind.

A nurse comes into the waiting room. We all sit up, suddenly alert. But the message is just that things are progressing. Jenny is nearly fully dilated, and the doctor thinks it won't be more than another hour or two.

I say a quick thank-You prayer on my way to the coffee pot. Carl and Tony head out for a stroll through the endless maze of corridors. As I watch them go, I remember all the avenues of help we tried. And how many of them were dead ends. And the years when father and son would not have walked anywhere together.

Another office, high in a tower. "I'm sorry," the psychologist said. "But you must realize that there's nothing I can do for Tony unless he wants help. I would suggest that you find someone to talk to yourselves, because you are the ones who need help." That wasn't what I wanted to hear. So I never went back.

I heard about a Christian woman counselor who was supposed to be very warm and kind, so I tried going to her next. She told me basically the same thing, but at least she said it more gently.

Tony did tell us that he'd get some help. He went to a counselor—once. "She helped me, Mom," he said. "I'm fine." We didn't know, so we believed him. I guess we wanted to.

A few months later, Carl pressed Tony a bit. "Where are you going with this?" he asked.

"I'm out of that life-style, Dad. Don't worry about it." We believed him—what did we know about being gay?

All during Tony's senior year in high school we believed

him. He dated occasionally, took girls to dances and the prom. Carl had shut the door; he felt Tony was over it and we should thank God. But deep inside, I knew it wasn't true.

Fall. We took Tony to the state university. He looked so lost, standing at the door of his dorm as we drove off. "I know all mothers have a hard time leaving the first one at college," I told Carl between mopping tears and blowing my nose. "But this is worse. How do we know what will happen to him there?"

I was right to be worried. Tony had problems fitting in. His roommate moved out after one semester. Tony didn't seem to have any friends. He struggled a lot, didn't come home, or write very often. When he did come home, he went out with people we didn't know. I know he went through stages, experimentation, trying to find out who he was. When I think about it, he must have been in a lot of pain. But I couldn't recognize his. And many of the things he went through I'm not sure I want to know about.

I suspected that he was not "over it," and I wondered what we had done wrong, why he couldn't get "fixed," what we would do if someone found out—on and on. It was like a living nightmare, like being in hell. They say hell is separation from God. Where is God in all this? I wondered. Why has He allowed this to happen to us?

Part of me kept saying, "Your son is probably gay, and it isn't going to go away," while another part said, "Ignore it and get on with your life and everything will turn out just fine because you are a Christian and it all will be okay."

And so our lives went on. But I died a thousand deaths; every time someone made a joke about "faggots" I cringed. I started looking at people differently, wondering if they were gay or straight. It was so hard to deal with that I finally just stuffed it all inside and went on as if nothing were wrong, hoping that the whole thing wasn't true.

After his third year, Tony dropped out of college and just drifted around the country, living in different cities, working at different jobs. We hoped he wasn't involved in the gay culture, but we didn't know. We heard from him now and then, but there was no closeness. He seemed very far away.

Everything came to a head one night in the grocery store when Carl ran into a friend of Tony's. "How's Tony doing?" the friend asked. "Is he still struggling so much with being gay?"

When Carl walked in, I knew by his white face and tight mouth that something was wrong. He told me what had happened. "It's not a big surprise," I said. "I've always known it inside."

At that point, we decided to find some help for ourselves since there didn't seem to be anything we could do for Tony. We went to one counselor who told us we had to tell the girls, that this was a family problem and we all needed to deal with it.

That was a big decision. We carefully told two people—a close friend and our new pastor—and asked them if they thought we should tell the girls. (Susan and Carrie were in college by that time, and Jenny was in high school.) They both thought we should.

It was so hard. We picked a Sunday after church when the girls were home for the weekend. We all sat down to lunch and Carl, slowly and carefully choosing his words, told them we had something we had to talk about.

"No, no," Jenny screamed. "It's not true. I know it's not true—it's a big lie." She ran from the room, the slam of her bedroom door echoed through the house.

I'd thought the older girls would be devastated and Jenny, who adored Tony and thought he was perfect, would roll with it. It was just the opposite. "Mom, Carrie and I suspected it anyway," Susan said. But I don't think Jenny ever got over that afternoon. I think it was one of the things that later pushed her into her own rebellious path in her teens.

The memory of that pain knots my stomach, and I squirm in my chair. All parents wish they could take their children's pain on their own shoulders. I'd be in there right now taking the pain of childbirth from Jenny if I could. But I can't. I can't now and I couldn't then. All I could do was to try to find someone else to help us. But it was hard because Jenny refused to talk about it; it was as though it didn't exist.

But God finally sent someone to help me—in a very strange way. In a Christian bookstore I found a book written by a Christian woman who had a gay son. Brave person that she was, she had included her phone number in the book.

"I know what you are going through," she said. "I've been there." She was right. She was the only person who understood.

She put me in touch with several other couples who were parents of gay children in our area, and we formed our own little support group. We called ourselves the Humpty Dumpties because our worlds had been shattered when our children told us they were gay. Nobody or nothing had been able to put us back together again—not all the king's horses or all the king's men—but the King Himself. He was the only one. Somehow or other God gives you the strength and brings you through to healing. But it's a very long, slow process.

After not hearing from Tony for nearly a year, one gray, chilly November day the phone rang.

"Mom, guess what? I've moved back to your area. I'm just an hour away. I'd like to come for a visit. But there's one thing—I'm living with this guy, Phil. He's important to me, and I want you to meet him. Can we come for a weekend?"

I called my Christian-author friend in a panic. "How can I deal with this? How am I supposed to handle his lover? I can't do it, I just can't."

"Connie, there's something you just have to understand. *It's your job to love him. It's God's job to change him.* Tony is an adult, and there's nothing you can do to change him. You did the best you could while you were raising him, you walked by the light you had, and now you have to take your hands off his life, leave him alone, and trust God." She pointed out that the story of the prodigal son is ultimately our hope because God always goes after the prodigal. "You can only trust that God will do that in His own way and in His own time," she said.

"Okay, I can accept and love Tony, but I don't think I can accept having his partner here—that's where I draw the line. That's just expecting too much."

"Connie," she said, "as much as he tells you this is a relationship that will last forever, it won't. They hardly ever do. And if you don't love him now—and love his friend—and leave their sin to God, then, when the relationship breaks up, he will not turn to you."

I knew she was right. After listening to her, we decided to make Tony's friend welcome in our home. "Okay," we told him, "but you can't sleep together here—that would be the rule even if it were a woman." I think he respected that. Tony and Phil spent time here, and later, we visited them and even stayed in their apartment.

We did it, but it was hard. Tony has to know how hard it was for us. Sometimes I worry that showing him love then was like putting approval on what he was doing. I hope he knew that wasn't true. It's hard to let someone know that you hate what he's doing but love him. But I think he understands even though we don't talk about it a lot.

My author friend proved to be very prophetic. A few months ago the phone rang again. Tony sounded so down I knew something was wrong. "Tony, is something bothering you?" I asked.

"Yeah, Mom. Phil and I split up. I'm feeling really low, even though it was my idea. Mom, do you think I could move home for a while? I really need to figure out what I'm doing with my life."

I thought about my writer friend, and I could almost hear her voice saying, "Connie, if you show him unconditional love now, when the relationship ends, he'll come back," and she was right.

Carl and Tony come back into the lounge. Tony's hair is mussed and he has a crease in the side of his face from sleeping on the edge of the plastic chair. I want to throw my arms around him and tell him again that I love him.

I don't know right now what God is doing in his life. I can only wait and see. There's a song called "I Care but Don't Mind" and I guess that describes me now. I care, I care a lot. I don't like what he was doing and perhaps still is. But I don't mind in the sense that I'm not bitter that it happened in our family, I'm not going off the deep end. I'm going to trust God that, like the prodigal son, Tony will come back out of the gay life-style.

I hate that word, "gay." It's not gay; it's anything but gay. It's painful and it's sinful and it's all kinds of things, but it's not gay. I know the gay world is a miserable world. There's a lot of disloyalty; gay relationships don't have a very good track record. I've never asked Tony how much he was, or is, into the promiscuous gay life-style. There are some things that are better not talked about, and I don't want to know.

AIDS is certainly something I think about. But I learned something from one of the women in the Humpty Dumpty group. She says that she prays daily for her son, that God would protect him from AIDS the way he protected Jonah while he was in the belly of the fish. And she believes that God can protect her son and she trusts him to do that. I believe that too. But if it happens, then God will get me through that too.

I spent years hiding the fact that Tony is gay. But even though I don't go around announcing it now, I'm trying not to hide it anymore. I just gave it to God and He's responsible. If He wants someone to know Tony is gay, that person will find out. And if it's going to help someone else, then fine. I don't think God wants me to spend my energy hiding it anymore.

I'm not sure where Tony is spiritually. One time I talked to him at length about my beliefs, and I said, "I wish I could wrap my faith and my love for God up in a package and give it to you so you could have it too." And he said, "Maybe deep down, way inside, I still do." And I let it go at that; we haven't talked about it since. Once in a while, on a holiday, he'll come to church with us. And every now and then, he'll ask me to pray for something.

Having a gay child isn't easy to accept. It's the hardest thing I've ever done. It's especially hard because homosexuality seems to be the one thing you can't talk about. I can share other problems with people, and I do, all the time. It's like therapy for me to talk to my friends, to pray together over problems, to share our feelings. But for a long time I couldn't talk about this. It's as if God gave me the one burden that I didn't feel I could share. During the years that I didn't tell anyone, I carried the heavy burden alone. But in a way it made me strong because when I couldn't talk to anyone but God, I talked to Him a lot. And somehow He always wrapped His arms around me and told me, "You are going to get through this." And I did.

The nurse comes in again. "We're moving her to the delivery room now. It shouldn't be much longer. Her husband is still with her. He says to say hi and tell you you'll soon be grandparents."

I picture Jenny in my mind: first the little girl, so tiny and fragile. It was so hard not to be overprotective because she was so little, so sick, so vulnerable, and needed me so much. It was hard to let go and stand back and let her go on her own. I'm not sure I ever really did, even after she had her surgery and her life became more nearly normal.

I picture the teenager, so cute with her infectious grin, big brown eyes, and long auburn curls. There were always boys hanging around our house.

But I also have to picture Jenny the rebel, those brown eyes flashing fire, screaming at me in fury, "Leave me alone, you can't tell me what to do anymore!" Angry words hurtling down hallways, doors slamming—they were regular sounds in our house.

Midway through kindergarten, Jenny's teacher had called and told me that Jenny wasn't really doing too well and she wasn't sure she should go on to first grade. But at the end of the year, she had made progress, so she was passed conditionally into first grade. And she did okay there. She had a superb teacher who took a lot of personal interest in her and helped her a lot. But as she progressed through the grades, it became apparent that she had problems. Looking back on it now, I know that she had learning disabilities that were never completely diagnosed and not diagnosed early enough. But she did get some help, and she managed to struggle through grade school, never doing really well but always doing well enough to pass.

What I didn't realize was that high school was going to be much different—harder and not offering nearly as much help. Jenny changed from a pleasant, happy little girl, who giggled and played Barbie dolls with her little friends, to being really insecure and unable to make the adjustment to the larger, more impersonal world of high school.

The farther she got into it, the more she rebelled. She wouldn't communicate with us; she resented us trying to help her with her homework. She made friends that weren't good for her—troubled kids from troubled backgrounds. We caught her in a lot of lies, and by the time she was a junior, I could see there were real emotional problems. We didn't know what to do. We started getting counseling at the high school, and it helped a little but didn't provide a solution.

Fortunately, Jenny never got into drugs and did only a small amount of drinking—I'm very grateful for that. Whatever the reason, God provided a shield that protected her from that.

She dated a lot, but sometimes her choices were not the best. At one point she was going with a boy we were never comfortable with, but we never knew why. Later we found out that he was from an abusive home and was physically abusing her. But she never told us. One night near the end of her junior year, I woke from a sound sleep, some instinct telling me that something wasn't right. I slipped out of bed and walked down the hall to Jenny's room—the bed was empty, the pink and white gingham spread still stretched neat and tight. I woke Carl in a panic. "Carl, Carl, it's 3:30 in the morning and Jenny's not home!"

We called all her friends, but no one knew where she was. I was absolutely desperate—I thought, She's dead. Every headline I'd ever read about every girl who was attacked ran through my mind. Even though I knew God had not deserted us, I also knew that we live in a real world and bad things happen to good people. I stayed up the rest of the night, crying and praying.

The next morning the phone finally rang—what a blessed sound! "Mom, I'm okay. I just didn't want to come home after the game." She'd spent the entire night wandering around the streets and had finally found a place to curl up and go to sleep.

At that point the high school counselor said we had to set some rules because we couldn't go through that again.

We sat down for a conference. "Jenny," we said, "if you ever do anything like that again you'll have to go to a foster home because we can't live like that anymore."

"Why are you making such a big deal of it?" she asked defiantly. "I'm not a kid. I can take care of myself." But I think she was scared, because for a while she was more cooperative.

But during her senior year things got really bad. Her grades were down, her self-image plummeted, and she started running around with some really bad kids. Her best friend was a girl who was expecting a baby. The girl's mother had been living with a string of men and her brother was a drug dealer. It was a bad situation, but I kept thinking, If we can just get her through this last year and graduated, everything will be much better. The pressure will be off, she'll get a job working with little kids like she loves to do, and everything will be fine.

But it didn't happen that way. The week before graduation she started dating a new boy, and after graduation she became even more rebellious. We tried everything—more rules, fewer rules, tears, pleading. Nothing worked. There was just constant fighting, constant "I'm 18 now and you can't tell me what to do."

A counselor's office again, a new one. It seemed like we had spent years of our lives in counselors' offices. "Jenny is a young adult now," she said. "You've modeled your values and beliefs to her for 18 years, and there's nothing more you can do. Jenny has to choose whether or not to follow them." I didn't want to hear that, but I knew she was right.

And Jenny chose.

"Jenny, where are you going and what time are you going to be back?" I asked as she grabbed the car keys and headed out the door.

"Mom, get off my back," she spit back. "Leave me alone. I'm tired of telling you every move I make." In a huff, she turned around, marched upstairs, packed her things, and moved out. She went to live with the pregnant high school friend.

I thought it would last just so long and then she'd come back, but I was wrong. Jenny never came back; she never slept overnight in our house again.

As the door slammed behind her, I just stood and sobbed. It was even worse than the night Tony told us he was gay. That night I still believed that we could get help and he'd change and everything would be okay again. This night I felt like my life was over.

I've had so many heartaches, I thought frantically, now my baby is moving out and this just hurts too much, I just can't take anymore. I actually ran out into the garage, thinking blindly that I was going to end my life by running the car with the door closed. But the garage was so full of junk there was no room to get the car inside!

Isn't this great, I thought. I'm such a failure I can't even get the car into the garage to commit suicide! I just had to laugh at myself. And, thank God, He removed those kinds of thoughts from my mind.

I thought Jenny was living with her friend and the girl's mother, but I found out that the mother had moved out to live with a man and left her pregnant 17-year-old daughter living alone. A few weeks later, Jenny's boyfriend, Dave, moved in.

That was another blow, but by then I had accepted the fact that she wasn't living a life-style of our choice. She was shaking her fist at us and at God, and while it hurt, it wasn't a big shock.

Our relationship was very strained. Jenny would call only if she needed a phone number or something. She never asked how we were; there was no communication.

One night several weeks after Dave had moved in, the phone rang. "Mom, I need my address book that's in the top drawer of my desk. Could Dad drop it off at Grandma's house? I can stop there after work."

I could hardly wait for Carl to get home. When I heard his tires crunch on the driveway, I hurried to the door. "What happened? How was she?"

"She was there, waiting for me. We didn't talk much, but she came so close to me a couple of times. I thought she wanted a hug. But I just couldn't. I cried all the way home," he admitted.

A day or two later, a good friend of mine from church, who knew about Jenny's moving out, called. She wanted to know how our relationship was going.

"We don't have a relationship," I said. "I don't talk to her."

"Why don't you go and visit her?"

"Visit her! I'm not going there. She's living in sin."

"Oh, and you've never sinned?" was her response. "You've never rebelled against God? And do you always make sure you approve of everything people do before you go into their house? Then you'd better not visit me because I've done some things you probably wouldn't approve of."

I started crying. "You're right," I sobbed. "I've been so wrong."

I picked up the phone and called Jenny and told her that her dad and I wanted to come over. She was dumbfounded and kept asking why. I told her that it was because we loved her and wanted to see her.

"What time do you want to come?" she asked. "I'll be here."

Their apartment was tiny, but immaculate. I sat on the edge of the tattered sofa. For the first 10 minutes I didn't say anything to Dave. Then I could hear my friend's voice in my ear, "And you didn't say anything to Dave? Is that reaching out to them?"

I finally blurted, "Hi, Dave, how are you?" And I thought, There, that's that. And I didn't say another word to him!

The next day Carl left on a week's hunting trip and I was alone—Susan and Carrie had gone back to college. I walked through that house and it seemed so big and so empty. I remembered the book by Judith Viorst, *Necessary Losses,* and I prayed, "Yes, they're necessary, but do they all have to come in one week? God, you've taken everything out of my life, and I can't stand it."

I didn't hear any voices or anything, but in a way it was almost as if God spoke to me that week, saying, "Aren't I enough for you?"

"No, You're not," I answered. "I need real flesh-and-blood people in my life. And I need joy and peace, and I don't have much of either right now."

I remembered a Bible study I'd been in years ago in which the leader told us that everything we have is a gift from God. "If you hold too tightly, God will pry your fingers open," she said. I began to think about that and to realize that I had to let God work in my life and let go of everything else.

As the week wore on and I spent a lot of time thinking and reading the Bible, God's Spirit gradually began to change my thinking. I began to see that God could get me through this, too, and use it for my good.

It won't be easy and it won't be painless, I thought, but I will get through it. And perhaps God will be able to use this in some way to help someone else. Maybe that person's pain won't be the same as mine, but pain is pain, heartbreak is heartbreak, and maybe God will be able to use it in His way.

It's strange, but when Carl left on his hunting trip I was depressed and miserable. And when he came back I had found some sort of peace. And so had he—he'd been with a good Christian buddy, and they had talked a lot, and he had thought and prayed a lot too. And that's when things began to heal.

We asked Jenny and Dave over for dinner and tried to make both of them welcome in our home.

Christmas Eve. Jenny's eyes glowed like the lights on the tree. "Look, Mom and Dad," she said, flashing a tiny diamond. "We're engaged." Carl and I didn't even mention that they were only 18 and both had only minimum-wage jobs.

We watched them struggle financially and in other ways those next months, but we worked very hard at not asking them about sensitive subjects and not giving them our opinion unless they asked for it. I tried not to be controlling in Jenny's life, and our relationship just grew and grew.

I struggle out of my heavy sweater—it's becoming very stuffy in the overheated lounge—and wad it behind my head to make a pillow.

A last picture comes into my mind. Jenny with the swollen belly of pregnancy. Still beautiful, still so tiny and fragile. In some ways that's my favorite mental snapshot of her.

My mind goes back for one final trip. I've nearly reached the end of the story God has made me replay in my mind as I wait for the final act of this little drama.

A gray day, spitting snow. By night we should have four to six inches, the weatherman said. I was too busy with my Saturday routine, planning the coming week for my in-home child care center, to notice the weather. I didn't even realize the doorbell had rung until Carl walked into the kitchen with Jenny and Dave.

"Mom, Dad," Jenny said in a subdued voice as she sank into the chair. "Guess what? You're going to be grandparents. We're having a baby."

That was a blow, to know our baby was having a baby and wasn't married. It was hard, but I love kids so much that the joy of knowing I was going to have a grandchild lit my heart. I'd been worried as Jenny was growing up that, because of all her physical problems, she wouldn't be able to have a baby. All Jenny's ever wanted was to be a wife and mother, so in some ways, this was an answer to prayer—even though it had come a little soon!

"That's wonderful," I managed after a moment's pause. And even as I said it, I realized it was true, this baby was a gift from God.

"We want to get married. I know it's short notice, but we'd like a little wedding. Would you help?"

Would we ever! It was small, but they had a lovely church wedding. Jenny was radiant in a creamy lace dress, Tony sang the Lord's Prayer, and we had a dinner for 20 people after the service.

"Mom," Jenny whispered to me as we were ready to leave. "Do you think I could work with you in your child care center? I could bring the baby after it's born."

Would I want that? You bet. Another answer to prayer.

"Is that it now, God?" I ask in silent prayer. "I've gone through it all. I've reviewed where we've come from. I'm not sure where we're going. Can I rest now?"

But God had one more thing for me to think about. I immersed myself again, one final time. "What," God made me ask myself, "have you learned from all this?"

I feel very hopeful when I think about all the things God has brought us through. Thirty years ago I could never have predicted what would happen. I would have thought we'd have the Ozzie-and-Harriet family. If someone had told me that it wasn't going to be that way—that I'd have a gay son and a rebellious daughter—I would have said, "But I don't want that. I can't go through that." But I did. And I still have so much to be grateful for.

God brought me through it. Carl and I have grown closer through it all and occasionally I've been able to help someone else.

One other thing I know came out of this for me—I

learned about not judging people. If I hadn't had trouble with my kids, I would have been so judgmental. I know I was when they were little and we weren't having any trouble with them. When I heard about someone else having trouble I'd think, Well, they must have done something wrong. I don't have any trouble. I was smart enough not to say it to anyone, but I *thought* it.

Going through troubles like ours gives you a lot of empathy for people who are in pain—it doesn't matter what kind of pain. God took away my attitude that, if you live a Christian life, everything will be fine and if it isn't, then you did something wrong. We're all sinners, we all do things wrong, and no one has the right to judge another person.

And despite everything, Carl and I are still able to have fun. Neither of us acts or looks (I think!) our age, and we can still giggle and have a great time.

There is life after pain, I thought—there's a lot of life: growing and learning and developing empathy for other people and becoming closer to God.

A shaft of light cuts the dim room as the door swings open. Jenny's doctor stands in the doorway, outlined in the glow. "Connie, Carl, you've got a granddaughter. A little girl—actually not so little, over seven pounds. She's gorgeous and Jenny's just fine."

Carl and Tony and I enfold each other in an embrace. I mop the tears away and head for the telephone to call Susan and Carrie.

An Encouraging Word

At some point during the challenge of family living, children change. The same children who captivated hearts with their endearing love and unquestioning compliance may become teens whose lives seem fueled by the need to rebel against their parents' traditional beliefs and values. As young parents cradle and kiss their infant children, they acknowledge that God will empower them, give them wisdom and strength, and guide them through whatever adversity may arise.

Connie's story allows us to glimpse into the lives of two devout parents who trusted their Lord, prayed for His guidance, and believed in God's promise of faithfulness. They rooted their children in the life of the church, intending to raise fine, upstanding children. As a result, when Tony and Jenny made decisions rejecting God's way for them, Connie was confused, aghast, and seemed to feel betrayed.

Are Christian parents exempt from disappointment and misfortune?

Occasionally, like Connie, we allow ourselves to believe that if only we will do everything the biblical way, everything will be just fine. Even when we are led to do God's will, as well as we understand it, the Christian life is not immune to tribulation. Sending children to parochial schools is surely God-pleasing but does not constitute an insurance policy against a child's sin or rebellion during the teen years. We have no promise from our Lord that the Christian's life will be free of worry, hurt, or despair. We do have His promise that He will stand with us.

Connie's expectation that she would have perfect children and a family free from any problems may have made it hard for her to be a careful observer of the small signals that her children were having difficulties.

Denial that problems exist prevents parents from working towards solutions.

Often, in an effort to assure ourselves that everything is really okay, we fail to notice early warnings and signs that problems are brewing. After all, if we can convince ourselves that nothing is the matter, we may be able to delay our confrontation with some painful realities.

Connie, for example, noticed that Tony was having difficulty "finding himself" and she made every effort to support him and encourage him. Nevertheless, she believed that Tony felt rejected by friends and was aware that parental reassurances weren't "sinking in." Tony had begun to do what he pleased, when he pleased, and shared little with his parents. Connie was resourceful, talking with friends, reading books about adolescent development, and sharing her concern with counselors at the high school and with her minister. Most of the advice she received tried to assure her that all boys go through a similar stage or that teenage rebellion often takes this form. For awhile, it seems as though Connie needed to believe that Tony could emerge unscathed from all his difficulties and the perfect life could continue undisrupted.

The pattern of denial is difficult for Connie to overcome. Even as Connie recalls Jenny's early years, we see many indicators that Jenny needed to have someone notice and attend to her imperfections. We are led to believe that Jenny had multiple undiagnosed learning disabilities and some early emotional problems. Perhaps Jenny sensed Mom's need to raise the perfect family and she may have been demoralized to realize that she could never give Mom a perfect little girl who earned perfect grades. As Jenny moved into the teen years she, like Tony, acted out her emotional pain by choosing poor friends, lying, and choosing to leave her family and live with a boyfriend. Connie returns to the belief that "if only we can get through this year, things will be much better." Her thinking is almost magical. Emotional problems that are continually denied can only fester without the healing influence of God's Law and Gospel and without the intervention of skilled helpers.

Many women believe it is more important to maintain peace in the household than it is to confront values or behaviors that are destructive. For many women, it is safer and simpler to retreat to the illusion that whatever the family's problem, it isn't as bad as it appears. As a result, some women become unknowing enablers of abusers, alcoholics, and conduct disordered teens. Whole families can become engaged in a conspiracy of silence, agreeing not to notice or discuss the family problem. Very often denial is an interval of waiting. Women ultimately wait until some family issue is so disruptive or hurtful that even confrontation is preferred to the ongoing dissonance. Ultimately, Connie confronts Tony because she can't suffer through the illusion any longer. And Tony, almost relieved to have an opportunity to share the truth, admits to his parents that he is gay.

Family members need to communicate openly with one another.

Connie revealed that after learning Tony was gay, she believed "there are some things better not talked about" and "some things I don't want to know." Connie also acknowledged that Jenny had not been able to talk with her parents about her boyfriend's physical abuse.

Parents need to establish a pattern of truth and sharing within the family. Children are left to deal with troublesome issues in isolation from family support and wisdom. And when long hidden truths are discovered, uninformed children feel very angry. Connie's daughters, especially Jenny, were upset to learn about Tony's sexual preference long after their parents knew about the issue. The girls were likely to have felt that their parents didn't trust them enough to tell them the truth. The girls probably felt that by withholding the facts, their parents had really been lying to them. When children aren't told the truth, they may wonder what else their parents

haven't told them or what other half-truths have been shared.
Every family should work hard to ensure that sharing with one another is a familiar and comfortable custom. Sharing begins with the simple tasks of communicating preferences and needs and reporting daily events. Such sharing builds the necessary trust that enables families to talk about dissonant issues in a healthy way with the confidence that their story will be heard with attention, compassion, and respect. Family business needs to be transacted openly, honestly, and in an age-appropriate manner with the children. Any concept can be communicated meaningfully to children in a fashion that will allow their understanding and their empathy. Whether that family business concerns divorce, economic difficulties, or value conflicts, all family members are entitled to hear the facts, learn every family member's opinions regarding the facts, and have a chance to share whatever feelings may be created by the facts.

The truth of the matter is that communicating is often the most difficult part of relationships today—between spouses as well as between children and their parents. When families realize that they can communicate more effectively, they may choose to seek a counselor who can help them talk together. Even those families who generally communicate rather well often struggle with the tasks of listening uncritically and nonjudgmentally during emotionally charged moments, when values conflict, or when adolescents and adult children are oppositional in attitude or behavior.

Establishing limits and communicating expectations about children's behavior is important.

Tony and Jenny did not wake up on any particular morning breathing the fire of adolescent rebellion. More likely, both Tony and Jenny had become progressively unhappy with themselves and more difficult for Connie to discipline. Connie acknowledged that it was difficult for her to set limits and say no. We assume that Connie did not talk with the children about her observations, her concerns, or her expectations for the children's behavior. The escalation of both teens' problems seems rooted in Connie's choice to overlook broken curfews, irresponsible behavior, and a disregard for God's will.

Parents communicate their love for a child by setting limits on the child's behavior. As a result, the child learns that the parents are strong, capable, and caring. A child must understand that there are meaningful consequences for inappropriate behavior. What better primer can a parent provide to help a child understand that "the wages of sin is death" (Rom. 6:23 NIV)? Children are expected to test the limits with great stamina and ingenuity, but they can trust that their parents have established limits that will prevent them from making too many hurtful mistakes. Love with control is perhaps one of the greatest contributions a parent can make to his or her child's development of a strong sense of self-esteem and psychological competence.

Parents may need to seek special help to deal with teens' rebellion.

Connie made some wonderful early efforts to deal with the information that Tony was gay. She did some reading to understand the issues more clearly, talked with high school counselors, shared her hurt with her minister, and relied on Christian friends for understanding and support. Connie also met with the parents of other gay children, which allowed her to understand that other parents have come through this problem, dealt with it, healed. This gave her hope that she could too. Talking with others who have a full understanding of our burden usually leaves us feeling less isolated, less shameful, and less helpless. Connie discovered, however, that her supportive friends and good listeners were not helping Tony.

When Connie did seek professional help, her earliest interactions with counselors disappointed her. Counselors told her that they weren't able to "fix" Tony or change him to meet Connie and Carl's expectations. They were candid in explaining that counseling is rarely effective if the counselee isn't seeking insight or change. When Connie learned that her son's homosexuality was likely to be a life-style preference as opposed to a temporary case of adolescent gender identity confusion, she never went back.

Connie believed herself to be a strong person. She recalled that when infant Jenny was small and ill and she didn't believe she could go on, "I did what I had to do." She recalled the feeling that she wanted to have a nervous breakdown but instead chose to "put one foot in front of another." Connie was not the kind of woman who collapsed under stress or feigned helplessness to get the attention and sympathy of others. Nevertheless, during this time, Connie recalls that the criticism of friends was contributing to her personal guilt and shame. She worried about others learning of Tony's life-style and became very aware of gay jokes. Her sensitivity to others' opinions of her began controlling her effort to reach out for support. She became so preoccupied with these concerns that she began looking at strangers, wondering if they were "gay or straight." She concluded that God had given her one burden that she couldn't share, and as a result, she carried much of that burden alone.

Often when we feel as though we are swimming up a waterfall and there is no one in whom we can confide, or from whom we can seek counsel, feelings of helplessness and personal surrender emerge. When Jenny moved out, Connie reported that her despair was so profound that she actually considered suicide as a means of escaping her pain. She felt as if God had taken everything from her. Connie desperately needed to hear her pastor or a counselor confirm to her God's promise that He is with her always. She needed a wise confessor to whom she could talk, as if speaking to God Himself. Her feelings of responsibility for Tony's and Jenny's decisions resulted in an oppressive sense of guilt and shame that cried out for a pronouncement of forgiveness, understanding, and the beginning of healing.

Once a Christian is reminded of God's unfailing love and faithfulness, psychological help can be very useful. If Connie had sought personal counseling, she would have learned that

Tony's life-style choice was influenced by heredity, hormone imbalances, brain chemistry, and childhood experiences. She would have been helped to feel that it would be difficult for Tony to change his sexual preference, yet comforted with the hope that, in God's time and with God's power, any life can be forgiven and transformed. And, very importantly, Connie would have been supported as she made decisions about how an adult parent responds to an adult child who has chosen a life-style that conflicts with God's will.

Parents must continue loving adult children who reject God's will and ways.
Very often it is easier to love someone of whom we disapprove when we realize how our heavenly Father continues to love us despite our own sin. As Christians, we seek the resolve to be penitent and ask for the forgiveness of our Lord whose death has atoned for all sins.

Connie struggled with the fear that by continuing to love her prodigal children, she might be communicating her approval of their behavior. She seemed to come to the understanding that efforts to encourage her children and not judge them will yield the most hopeful results. Connie conquered personal uncertainty when she invited Tony's friend Phil to the house and again when she tried to make Jenny and Dave comfortable in her home at dinner. She followed the example of Jesus, giving love, without approving of the "sinners" and tax collectors of His time.

Connie might have made the choice to sever her relationship with her children. Some very devout Christian parents have done precisely that with the hope that their children would choose their parents' approval and repent of the sinful behaviors to which they had succumbed. Most parents lose their adult children for years, decades, or forever as a result of that decision. Connie's choice to continue demonstrating her love for Tony and Jenny enables her to remain in relationship with them. It is a remarkable victory for Connie to have reached the point where she can say, "I don't necessarily share my adult children's values, but we are there to support one another in our journey through life." Connie and Tony were sitting together awaiting the birth of Jenny's child. Jenny ultimately chose to marry her boyfriend and begin to accept God's way for her and her newborn. Connie will never know to what extent her presence, counsel, and love encouraged Jenny to make God-pleasing decisions. As Connie continues to pray for God's will to be done in Tony's life, she continues to love her son. Connie must still wrestle with some of her irrational beliefs, however. She cannot hold God accountable for "rescuing Tony," for as He has the rest of us, God has given Tony free will. And Connie cannot hold God responsible for her expectation that "God will protect Tony from AIDS." Connie will need to work hard to understand that Tony's sexual decisions have life-threatening consequences for which he must accept personal responsibility.

Perhaps Connie can encourage Tony to seek professional help to acquire insight and an objective perspective about his life-style decisions. Tony must be helped to bear his burden, hopefully with compassionate counsel that may enable him to understand his homosexuality and lead him to repentance and reliance on God's help to grow in newness of life.

Trust God's wisdom and faithfulness.

As we review Connie's story, we can see how her reliance on God supported her through very difficult family moments. Connie concludes her story by sharing that she has learned to have empathy for people in pain and that there is life after the kind of pain and uncertainty she experienced. Connie shares, "We're all sinners, we all do things wrong, and no one has the right to judge another person." Those are powerful statements from a woman whose adult children have rejected her deepest beliefs and have made decisions contrary to God's will. Connie fears not only for her children's well-being now, but she also fears for their eternal well-being.

We may all take comfort in the knowledge that the Holy Spirit continues knocking at each heart's door, working to give the gift of faith. And each of us, like Connie, needs to come to the realization that trusting God's wisdom and faithfulness to prevail is the wisest choice any parent can make.

Beverly K. Yahnke

Guidelines for Handling Value Conflicts

- Communicate. If your family has a pattern of candidly and openly sharing with each other feelings, preferences, and facts about their lives, your family will handle dissonance between members in a healthy way. If you do not communicate well, it would probably be helpful to seek out a counselor who can help you talk. The fundamental building blocks of communication are often neglected during value conflicts.
- Trust. Without a sense of trust, communication can't go very far. Work from the earliest stages of family life to develop a sense that it's okay to say what you think and feel within the family because the others will listen, understand, and use the information shared in everyone's best interests. And make that trust especially clear during value conflicts.
- Respect. Whenever two adults are involved, there must be mutual respect, not only from child to parent but also from parent to child, treating the child as another adult. Too often parents want only to communicate their own values and don't want to listen to what their adult children think and feel.
- Accept. As a parent you need to accept your child where he or she is. Parents risk losing their relationship with their child permanently if they cannot accept the person, even while not accepting his or her actions.
- Don't deny. Closing your eyes to a problem and pre-

tending it doesn't exist may help you deal with immediate pain, but in the long run it is destructive to you and to the adult child whose behavior you are denying.

- Let go. When the little bird is in the nest you take care of it, teach it to fly, and pick it up when it falls. But when the big bird is ready to fly, you can only stand with your heart in your mouth hoping that God has given you enough wisdom to have done your job and say goodbye. Parents must reach the point where they say, "You are on your own now. I will respect the decisions you make and not try to tell you what to do any longer because I love you enough to let you live your own life."
- Prevent. Look for red flags early in family life. When you see little problems, don't deny that they exist but acknowledge them in a positive way, seeking outside help when necessary. Working to solve little problems goes a long way to preventing them from becoming big ones.
- Trust God. It's especially hard when adult children reject their parents' deepest beliefs and forsake God and Jesus Christ as their Savior. Then parents fear not only for their child's happiness in this world but also for his or her soul. In that case, parents can only look to the story of the prodigal son and remember that God continues to present Himself to adult children in many ways. The Holy Spirit will continue knocking on the door of that child's heart. But you must accept that there is nothing you can do to instill faith in your child. Trusting that God's wisdom will prevail is the wisest choice a parent can make.

Reflection

- At what point in her story did you feel the most empathy for Connie?
- For you, what would be the most painful reality to face? That your son or daughter was homosexual? That your son or daughter was living in a sexual relationship outside of marriage? Something else?
- For some reason, conflicts over sexual values seem to be especially difficult for many families to handle. Why do you think this is? Do parents have the right to insist that their sexual values be followed in their home?
- For a long time, Connie lived with "this horrible thing always in the back of my mind." Why do you think Christians are reluctant to admit family/personal problems to others and seek help?
- Do you agree that being a perfectionistic parent is destructive? Why or why not? In what ways do you think unrealistic expectations in family life can cause strain?
- Rebellion and rejection hurt parents deeply. In what way has loving your children made you vulnerable? What did you find in Connie's story that encouraged you to continue searching, loving, and forgiving?
- When you were younger, how did you envision your future life and family? Were your expectations fulfilled? What has God taught you through the unexpected over the years?
- If you had been the parent of the child in Luke 15:11–32, how might you have reacted? What advice might you have for other parents based on your experience? (Note another troubled family in 2 Sam. 13:1–19:4.)

Heavenly Father,
I'm not perfect.
Please forgive me.
Draw me back
beneath Your
protection and care.

In parenting my children,
help me remember the way
You are parenting me.

Guide me.
Make me strong
and wise
and reliant on Your mercy.

Keep my children in the palm of Your hand.

And Father, too,
when other parents struggle,
help me find a way
to ease their burden
as Your mercy eases mine.

Amen.

Story 4

Ruth: Time Enough

by Annette Frank

Ruth

So Ruth gleaned in the field until evening. (Ruth 2:17 NIV)

There is a time for everything, and a season for every activity under heaven. (Eccl. 3:1 NIV)

What a beautiful fall morning! A perfect morning really—wispy clouds in a turquoise blue sky. I love sitting out here on the deck. The dogwood is so beautiful this year. I don't ever remember seeing the leaves such a brilliant red. And look how big it is! Phil planted that tree when Josh was just a few months old. The air seems so clear. Feels great to breathe it in. There's a bit of a chill in it—soon it'll be sweater weather. How quiet it is. Even the neighborhood dogs aren't barking—talk about a miracle! I should do this more often. Wish I had *time* to do this more often.

Tranquility. Peace. Calm. What a *contrast* to the way my life sometimes seems. There are days when I've felt I was in a race car barrelling down a track, hardly able to glimpse a passing flag. Sometimes I've felt I was on the sideline watching life race past me. Would it help if I yelled, "Help, God, life seems out of control. It's all too fast, too much happening!"

We're just into fall activities and already the feeling of being carried along in the mad dash is a bit overwhelming. Drive the children to school activities, pick up someone from practice, drive to games, off to the shopping mall for school clothes, off to church for Sunday school teachers meetings. Before you know, it'll be time to practice with my class for the Christmas Sunday school service! Then there's my work at the office and business meetings. My stomach starts twisting just thinking about it. Is that what it's all about: meetings and running around? Whatever happened to the quiet life?

Well, I'm going to enjoy these few moments to myself before Phil and the children are up and it'll be time for the usual Saturday tasks. What is that passage from Ecclesiastes? "There will be a time for every activity, a time for every deed." I think that's true. I could panic thinking about all there is to do, but what purpose would that serve—just make me feel anxious and who needs to add more to the old stress level. It's better to just take one thing at a time as Ecclesiastes implies.

It does seem to me things were calmer when the children were little. They weren't involved in all those school and church activities. With life whizzing past at this rate, they'll be in college soon or even starting families.

Guess they'll be facing many of the same decisions Phil and I, and also our parents, have over the years. I wonder if Rachel will be able to be—or choose to be—a stay-at-home mom, at least at first. What a major decision that was for Phil and me. It was something we thought about even before Rachel, and later Joshua, came into our lives. I wonder if it was a hard decision for our folks to make since both sets of parents worked.

Phil's mom still takes care of children in her home. She's been able to stay at home, which has always been a priority, and yet she has an income. With her love of children, this has been perfect for her. She's doing something worthwhile and special for the children she cares for—as well as the working parents.

Mother still does part-time bookkeeping. Where Phil's mom loves her children, Mother loves her books and figures. She'll never retire. She's always enjoyed her job, and her company is good to her. I don't ever remember a time when she didn't work at May's. Today my career is important to me also. But when Phil and I were married, we agreed I should stay at home with the children. That was a good decision. I remember that conversation.

"Ruth, when the children come I think you should stay at home with them. I remember coming home to the smell of cookies baking or brownies waiting for us. And Mom always had a hot meal. She still remembers all of us kids banging through the door after school and searching the kitchen for signs of dinner. It always smelled so good. I want those kinds of memories for our children."

"I know. I'd like to be at home with the children—at least until they're in school. I want to be the one to help them learn to take care of themselves. My mother must have been at home when we were really little, but I remember being a latch-key kid. I don't think as children we ever minded taking care of ourselves after school. But there are some things I think I missed. I've always thought it would be so neat to work in the kitchen with a daughter—you know—cutting up lettuce or mixing cookies. I think I learned fractions mixing cookie dough—a half cup of butter and a cup of sugar. I want cookies made by a mother-child *team!*

"But, Phil, it concerns me how we'll manage on one salary. It's been difficult sometimes with just the two of us. It's not that we're living extravagantly; it's just that house payments and everyday needs take so much, and then we still have your student loan. Some day the car will have to be replaced, and we can't seem to find a way to save ahead for that."

"We shouldn't wait forever to be parents, though, Ruth. I'd like to be able to play baseball and basketball with a son—we will have a son, won't we? You could show him how to make cookies. But I don't want to wait until we can *afford* children. I'll be Abraham's age if we do that! I want to be able to do things with my children. Rocking chairs are fine for dads with babies, but I'd like to play with my children. And I know how much you love children.

"I can get a different job, one that pays more. Or I can

look for a second job. I just don't think we should have children and then send them off for someone else to raise. True, there are wonderful sitters like Mom, but I just think if God gives us children, we should raise them."

"Honey, I agree. Children *are* special. And we should care for them. But teaching is more than a full-time job. You're always doing lesson plans, grading papers, looking for new ideas for your classes, making things for your classroom. When would you ever have time for a second job? You leave for school at 7:30 in the morning. You don't get home until after five o'clock in the evening.

"And what kind of family life would we have if you took a second job? Why, I'd never see you, and when would you enjoy any child God gave us? How could you ever be the father to a child if you were never home except to sleep and change clothes? Besides you'd be a big grouch because you'd always be tired. Teaching is more than enough to do."

"Ruth, I love you. I'll love any child we'll have. I'll do anything for you and anything to enable you to stay home with our children."

"Let's keep thinking and praying about this, Phil. I'm sure God has something in mind. We need to continue to place our cares and concerns on Him. He's always shown us the way in the past."

Phil sure takes his responsibility as a provider seriously. He felt inadequate in the early days of our marriage, and I think it still bothers him that without my salary we just wouldn't make it. It doesn't matter that we live very modestly. Clothes are expensive. Food bills get bigger, especially as Josh becomes older. Insurance rates have gone up. Taxes are greater. Phil's a wonderful provider. And he has such a gift for teaching, he *should* be teaching, even if he thinks it doesn't pay enough.

God sure gave us reassuring messages about our financial concerns and our decision that I would be a stay-at-home mom while the children were young. God put "billboards" on the road, highlighted with flashing neon lights! Right before Rachel was born, we heard a sermon based on God's request that Abraham sacrifice Isaac—a test of Abraham's love for God. Isaac wondered where they would get the animal to offer to the Lord, and Abraham said, "God will provide." The sermon in church that Sunday was based on those words of Abraham. Just to be sure we got the message, we heard it again through music in a concert we attended that same evening. We knew that our finances would always be tight and there would be sacrifices to be made, but we also knew that God had promised us, "I will provide." As I think about it, we were—and are—in somewhat the same situation as Abraham. Abraham trusted God to take care of Isaac, and we trust God to provide for Rachel and Josh—as well as the two of us.

Through the years, we've sometimes wondered just *how* God would provide and have been amazed at His methods. I remember when Josh was about 18 months and Rachel was 3, we ran out of money several days before payday.

"Ruth, we need milk and there's no cereal. Looks like we're at the end of the bread. Do we ever have enough peanut butter? I'll stop on my way home from church voters' meeting tonight and get at least milk and cereal."

"Okay. Do you have any money? I used the last of the grocery money a couple of days ago."

"I had to get gas for the car so all I have is a dollar."

"Let's see if there's some loose change around. Try your pants pockets, and I'll check out my coat."

I don't remember where we came up with the extra change, but Phil brought home milk and cereal. We did some hard praying. How were we going to manage until payday? We've always planned menus and budgeted very carefully and used all kinds of coupons. But that time we just didn't make it. I really thought about getting a job, but then what would happen to Josh and Rachel? God answered our prayers. He reminded us that when He promised to care for us, He'd provide.

We had a phone call from our bachelor neighbor, Carl. "Ruth, this is Carl. My sister just called. She's injured her eye and will be in the hospital a few days. After she gets home she'll need someone to care for her for awhile, so I'm driving out to stay with her."

"Oh, Carl, I'm so sorry to hear about your sister. We'll keep you both in our prayers. Is there anything we can do? Should we pick up your mail? Water your plants? Anything?"

"Thanks, Ruth, I'd appreciate all that. Would you mind if I brought over some groceries? I just went shopping and have milk, meat, fruit, and other things that won't keep until I get back. It would be a shame for them to spoil. Could you use them?"

Thinking of that, I am still amazed at God's goodness. Phil was so surprised at having steak for dinner that night. He couldn't get over how he had left for school wondering if he should get a better-paying job or at least a part-time one—or even take out a loan—and he came home to a refrigerator full of food and a steak for dinner!

And God did provide a part-time job for me a few months later. My friend Laura, then a law student, now a successful lawyer, had a classmate who was blind and needed people to read class materials for her. The government paid for readers and provided the taping equipment. I got the reading job! I'd read some of the most interesting cases and other law-related material at night when the children were in bed. Laura would pick up the tapes and materials in the morning on her way to law school and drop off new tapes and new reading assignments. Because Phil would be at meetings or doing school-related work most nights, I was able to read without interfering with my other responsibilities. And it was wonderfully stimulating!

We've been really blessed over the years. I know there are women who had their babies and six weeks later went back to work rather than give up a life-style they'd come to enjoy. Laura, for example. I recall when her first child was born and how much she enjoyed being at home taking care of that sweet little girl. You could tell this was the ultimate experience for her. And the tears she shed as she thought about leaving her! She found a wonderful older woman who cared for two other infants. But Laura missed Emily's first step and shared the title of "Ma" with the sitter for a long time.

It was a struggle for Laura to give up being a stay-at-home mom. But her law career was finally doing well. She was in a firm she really liked. If she stayed at home with Emily, she'd give up the years she'd put in establishing herself. The family would have had to move to a smaller home. She'd have had to give up her cleaning person—no small thing for Laura. I don't think it was so hard for her to go back to work after her boys were born. She seemed resigned to it.

Laura would say she has to work. She's working for many of the same reasons we all work: the bare necessities of life— a roof over our heads, food, clothing. And the things we value: a quality education for our children, and yes, for ourselves too, reliable transportation, a chance to visit our families that are so far away. I guess some day we might work to save for our old age. I guess what Laura sees as a need is different than what I see as a need. But I'm glad she can accept my life-style and my values as being what God has in mind for me.

A lot of women don't have a choice about working. They have to earn a living. It isn't a matter of choice. My neighbor Susan has that darling little boy, Mike, and a full-time job. She doesn't make much as a secretary and has all the expense of raising a child and providing a home for him. Knowing our money struggles, I wonder how she manages. There isn't a second provider. She has all the child-care expenses for Mike. I know she'd like to move into a larger apartment, especially when Mike gets older. I wonder if she gets help from her family?

Thank God for family! How nice it was to receive those "care packages" with new and reusable clothes when the children were smaller. Dear Mother, she'd always try to include a little toy or special hair ribbons—something "fun" for each child. And Aunt Barbara, with no children of her own, has always treated Rachel and Joshua like grandchildren. She has such a knack for always getting them just the right "in" things. If Mike were older, we could share some of Josh's outgrown clothes with him. By the time he's big enough to wear Josh's clothes, they'll be out of style. Of course, Josh usually wears his clothes to death so there's very little to share, even with the clothing barrel at church.

We do seem to be concerned about money. I don't think we're trying to "keep up with the Joneses." It's just that day-to-day existence is costly—so I guess I'll keep on sharing the provider role with Phil.

It seems ages ago I thought about returning to work. I remember Josh was going into first grade. We decided after he had been in first grade for a couple of months, I'd look for a job. Why were we concerned that he might not make it? That little blond 6-year-old had all his supplies carefully placed in his book bag days before the opening of school. He even packed his lunch a couple of days early! Oh, the odor coming from his bag! We discovered it was a salami sandwich. Today we'd think it was his gym shoes!

The first few days of that school year seem so calm as I realize what's going on in our life now and what's coming up in the days, weeks, and months ahead. Back then I'd get up and make breakfast for everyone. Phil and the children would drive off to school. It was nice they all were in the same school. The children stayed with Phil after school. (That had many unplanned benefits. The children learned to do their homework while waiting for Daddy. And then they could go out on the playground for some recreation before heading home.)

I'd have dinner ready, and we'd have a nice calm dinner hour, followed by devotions. We had time for games and stories in the evenings—well, maybe not all four of us. Phil and I agreed that as long as the children were in school, at least one of us would be home in the evening. We did have some wonderful bonding time.

My feelings of *that* kind of calm were short lived. It came time to "pound the pavement" as they say. Actually, I'd been thinking about what kind of job I'd like for awhile. After eight years of being at home, I had some doubts. How would I find a job? If someone hired me, could I do the work? What was this going to do for our family life? The only thing I really knew was that I wanted to be in a situation where I could share Jesus. I wanted to find a job where somehow God would use my talents and I could serve *Him*. True, I became preoccupied with money concerns—even after all the assurances that He would provide—but deep in my heart, I wanted to serve the Lord.

It isn't easy to see how real estate banking is serving the Lord. However, over the years He's shown me how to share Him with our clients at times when they needed the reassurance of God's love. I think, for now, God has me where He wants me.

It sure is pleasant out here on the deck. It's so relaxing. There was a time, though, when Saturday mornings were not my favorite time. That was back when I was reading for the blind student. I get tired now, but I was really tired for a while back then. That's probably how Susan feels.

"Ruth, some days I'm so tired when I get home. My boss is so demanding. I barely get one thing done when there's something else to do. And she's such a perfectionist that I'm afraid to make a mistake. I feel like I always have to be on my toes. By the time I pick up Mike, I'm exhausted. I feel guilty when he asks me to play with him and I say no. He can't understand I work hard all day and then have to come home to make dinner and clean things up and get clothes ready for the next day. He has so much energy and wants to play. But I'm dragging. What kind of relationship is it when I get crabby through the evening? I hate it when I lose it! It isn't his fault I'm tired, yet he's the one that feels the effects of my fatigue and frustration."

Boy, do I know how she feels! I remember only too well Saturday mornings after I started my reading job. It seemed that Rachel and Joshua were always up at the crack of dawn, and Saturday was no exception. I'd get up with them, and we'd find quiet things to do so Phil could sleep late. Sometimes I'd be so tired that I'd fall asleep reading to them only to be wakened by "Mommy! Mommy, what happened to the rabbit? Are you sleeping, Mommy?" It seemed that we read every book we owned. I tried not to complain, but I'm sure I was a real grouch all day.

Then there was the Saturday I just couldn't take it any longer. I was reading with the children. We were sitting on the sofa. Phil came in and all he said was, "Good morning everyone!" I remember saying, "What's good about it?" and a tirade of words followed. Those three must have been very surprised. I don't ever remember being so upset. I do remember finishing whatever it was I said, going to the bathroom, slamming the door, and having a good cry. When I felt better, I came out to three very quiet people who suggested I go back to bed. I did.

Several nights later, after the children were in bed, Phil asked, "Ruth, what about Saturday morning?"

"I'm sorry. I guess I was just tired. Forgive me?"

"You're already forgiven, but what about Saturdays? I never realized it bothered you that I'd sleep late on Saturdays while you got up with the kids. You've always been an early riser, so I didn't think a thing about sleeping a little later when you'd get up."

"It's just that I get so tired sometimes. I'm up early with the children *every* morning. I really love being at home with them, but they're so active! I get tired sometimes. And it seems that a couple of times a week the reading assignments I get are longer, so I stay up and read while you go off to bed. ... Before you say anything, I'm not complaining. I enjoy the reading. It's usually interesting. Who knows, maybe some day I can study law. ... Don't look at me like that! Anyway, the extra income really helps. Let's just forget it, okay?"

"Ruth, obviously this is bothering you. I could hear your resentment, frustration, and anger last Saturday morning. We need to talk about this. We need to do something about it."

"What about Saturday mornings?"

"What would you like on Saturdays?"

"To sleep later."

"Okay."

"But I can't. You need the rest, Phil, and the children need attention."

"Do they make tranquilizers for kids?"

"Oh, Phil!"

"I didn't mean that. But do they? Smile, Ruthie, it's just a joke. I'll get up Saturdays and you sleep late."

"No. You really need that extra rest or *you'll* be grouchy! Too bad we don't have family closer who'd take the children over a Friday night once in awhile."

"Yeah, I know two grandmothers who'd give anything for that opportunity. But it'd be a little extravagant to fly Rachel and Joshua out to a grandmother so we could both sleep late."

"Maybe we could take turns sleeping in."

"You get the first and third Saturdays and I get the second and fourth?"

"Right. If there's a fifth all four of us sleep in."

"Sounds good to me, but I can't imagine those two early birds doing that! Their inner alarm clocks go off at dawn."

Actually, we had the answer almost immediately. It was as if God opened our eyes to see what was happening in our family.

When did Rachel and Josh begin helping with mealtimes? Seems they always were there to put the napkins on the table or arrange the silverware. It was one of those mommy-children things I always wanted to do with Mother. It did seem they always wanted to help, so we'd do things together. It was from this that Phil noticed how independent they had become.

"Ruth, look how the children help you at mealtime. Why, Rachel can even pour the milk when the container isn't real full. And Josh does a good job of smearing jam on bread, table, napkin, and self."

"He is getting better. They are good helpers. Sometimes it takes a little patience to allow them to help because I could do something faster, but how will they learn to take care of themselves if I always do everything? Besides, we do have fun around the house. At least we try to make it fun. Remember what you told me when you were student teaching? 'A happy child is a learning child.' I've really thought about that a lot through the years."

"Well, I've thought of a way to make them ecstatic since they do like to help so much."

"Oh?"

"Why couldn't they take care of themselves on Saturday mornings?"

"Phil, they're so young. But ... they do seem to be able to do things pretty well."

"We'd probably have to do things in little steps so it wouldn't seem so overwhelming to them."

"Let's talk to them about this."

"Sounds good to me. How about tomorrow right after devotions. We might even begin the Saturday Morning Game Plan in a couple of weeks. In the meantime, this Saturday *you* sleep late—just for the practice—and *I'll* fall asleep reading to those two early birds."

We had our family meeting after devotions that next night. Phil read the Bible story of Jesus washing the disciples' feet, and we talked about serving each other and doing things that were helpful.

"Rachel, I want to thank you for being such a helpful big sister to Joshua," Phil began. "I like how you show him how to do things and help him do something well. And Josh, I like how you try to do things and do a good job. I've been watching you both help Mommy at mealtimes. Rachel, I like having the napkins folded differently at every meal. And Josh, you do a good job of lining up the fork, knife, and spoon at everyone's plate. I especially appreciate how neatly you both eat."

"I agree with your daddy. You both are very helpful around the house. You help make your beds. You pick up your toys. Josh, you're getting real good at toy-basketball. And Rachel, thanks for lining up all our shoes in the closet so nicely."

"How would you two like a special grown-up thing to do? Remember how tired Mommy was last weekend? Well, if you two would be able to get up and play quietly by yourselves for a little while on Saturday mornings, Mommy could sleep a little later—just like I do. How does that sound to you? Want to give it a try?"

"Daddy, I could make breakfast. Josh, you could help."

"Can we have jelly sammiches?" (Josh still likes jelly sammiches.)

"Daddy, I can make sandwiches with lids on them."

That settled it. We put the Saturday Morning Game Plan into action. Actually it started Friday evenings before Josh and Rachel went to bed. In the kitchen we'd put two bowls on the table, pull all the boxes of cereal close to the edge of the pantry shelf, place the bread and toaster near the edge of the counter (maybe the toaster came when they were a little older), set the margarine and jelly on the table, and pour two glasses of milk that were put on the bottom shelf of the refrigerator. Everything was within Rachel and Josh's reach.

Saturday morning they were up with the birds as usual. The first couple of Saturdays Phil and I took turns checking on them—hopefully without their knowing. They acted so grown up being quiet and getting breakfast by themselves. Of course, we had our usual Saturday brunch later.

Really, the Saturday Morning Game Plan was good for them as well as for me. They learned to depend on themselves. I learned they could get along without me—early steps toward "cutting the apron strings."

I'll have to share the Saturday Morning Game Plan with Susan. Maybe she wouldn't want Mike to make his own

137

breakfast, but they could prepare a snack for him for Saturday morning, and perhaps he wouldn't mind playing quietly by himself for awhile. I wonder if he'd like to spend a Friday night with us. Maybe we could try one of our family pajama parties. We haven't done one of those in years.

When the children were younger Friday was family night. I always tried to schedule a fun meal—tacos, fancy hot dogs, pizza. Some nights we'd watch a special television program. If it was a baseball game, Josh would like to have his hot dogs during the game—just like at the ball park.

Somewhere along the line, Rachel was invited to a slumber party and had such a good time, she cooked up a family slumber party. We'd all get ready for bed early. Rachel and Josh would get out their sleeping bags and have them in the family room. We'd order pizza and have pizza and soda picnic style in the family room. When it was time to go to bed, Josh and Rachel would roll out their sleeping bags and Phil and I would sleep on the sleeper couch. Sometimes Phil and I wouldn't be quite ready to sleep, but it was such fun talking to everyone with the lights out. Sometimes we'd be laughing so hard Phil and I wondered if our old recycled couch would make it through the night. It sure squeaked a lot when we moved. Of course, we'd all laugh louder thinking Mom and Dad were falling through the bed.

Family slumber parties aren't practical any more. Now Rachel usually works Friday and Saturday evenings. Josh very often has friends over Fridays or is at a friend's if he doesn't have a game.

Time. Seems like there never is enough time to do everything we'd like to do. If we didn't schedule Sunday nights as family night, we could easily lose touch with one another. Breakfast together doesn't work anymore because I have to leave earlier than anyone else, and I think they all need those extra minutes of sleep in the morning. Thankfully, we can still have a family dinnertime most evenings. But we'll have to really hang on to Sunday evenings together—even if it isn't the whole evening. We've already shared "our" time with a couple of Rachel's dates. It's nice that she thinks being a family is important enough to be home on Sunday evening—even if it means cutting a date short. I expect she'll want to give up bussing one of these days so she can have a more normal social life. Maybe our Sunday evenings will be more *ours* then.

We try to keep to a schedule for our family life. Even our mealtimes are scheduled, right down to the food. I'm not particularly fond of planning menus. In fact, I like planning menus about as much as Phil likes paying bills and balancing checkbooks. We seem to schedule those activities for the same night. Now the children take part in the planning. That came about as a kind of accident. Like the Saturday Morning Game Plan, I can see the Lord leading us again and for many of the same reasons.

"Oh, give thanks unto the Lord, for He is good, and His mercy endures forever."

"Rachel, is it your turn to wash the pots or Josh's?"

"I think it's mine, Mom. Josh, don't drop the butter. Josh, why don't I clear the table and load the dishwasher, and you wash and dry the pots?"

"I'll load the dishwasher, you wash the pots, and Mom and Dad have almost cleared the table."

"Phil, what are your plans for tonight?"

"I'm going to pay the bills."

"Josh, Dad's going to pay the bills. Mom, can I go to Ann's house? shopping? to the library? lock myself in my room?"

"No wonder we had pie—CHERRY pie—for dessert. I thought there was something fishy. Rachel, can I go to Ann's with you? What am I saying! I must be desperate! Mom, can I go to Jeff's or Matt's? Do you think they'd let me stay overnight? The library. That's it. Can I go to the library?"

"All right you two, that's enough."

"But Dad, you get so grumpy when you do the bills."

"Yeah, Dad. Rachel's right. Whenever you work on the bills, you jump all over us. 'Josh, turn down the TV.' 'Josh, why did your mother give you five dollars for school?' 'Josh, did you give your offerings this month?' Everything seems like a federal case."

"Leave your father alone. He's not really getting irritated with you. He's irritated with the situation."

"But, Mom, he always acts like it's our fault he has to pay the bills. Why don't you pay the bills? Or let Rachel pay them. She's always spending money!"

"And I suppose you don't, brother dear? Who just needed a new pair of soccer shoes? And who didn't have any blue jeans to wear? And who *had* to have a jacket so he wouldn't freeze to death—and it's almost 70 degrees out."

"Enough! Now that your dad and I have cleaned up the kitchen, who's going to wash and who's going to dry the pots? What happened to the schedule we had on the calendar? Rachel, see if the calendar's in the drawer."

"Ha! Josh, *you* get to wash the pots."

"While you *two* are washing and drying the pots, you can help me with next month's menus!"

"Oh, no! Rachel, call Ann. Ask her if we can move in for a few days! Mom's doing the menus."

"Josh!"

"Mom, come on! You know how you get when you do menus. Okay! Okay! You don't have to look at me that way!"

"If you don't like my attitude about menu planning, why don't you help. In fact, I think it's a great idea. You get to choose meals you like. Josh, you can plan Friday night meals and Rachel, you plan a meal for each week. They can be simple. In fact, the easier the better."

"Is Dad going to plan a meal a week for a month also? And I can guess what Josh will plan."

"Your father always asks for meatloaf—ground turkey, of course—baked potatoes, and a tossed salad when I ask him. He also asks for cherry pie. But he'll be through with bill paying by then so we'll skip the cherry pie until his birthday.

"Josh, any ideas as to what you want? Remember, they have to be balanced meals. A banana split does not count as a balanced meal."

"I'm ready. Pizza. Ravioli. Spaghetti. Tacos."

"Oh, brother! Mom, that's all he ever wants. And we can have frozen pizza. We don't have to order out if we don't have the money. We can have frozen ravioli. I like the kind in the white box with the red letters. Plenty of sauce. Get an extra container, okay? And don't make spaghetti. I like the kind in the bottle better. It doesn't have all those chunks of soggy tomatoes. And I'll warm the taco shells when we have tacos. That'll help you Mom, right?"

"Some help. Josh ..."

"No, Mom. Those are the menus I planned. They're nutritious. Pizza has cheese—dairy group; meat—protein; tomato sauce—vegetables; crust—grains. Some part of it has to be carbohydrates. Ravioli and spaghetti are the same. And if we *have* to—add a salad bar. But I'm not eating that green stuff that looks like bushes! And forget the 'fungus among us'!"

"I like mushrooms! Mom, all he ever wants is pizza, ravioli, spaghetti. Josh, why don't you move to Italy!"

"This isn't getting the menus planned. Rachel, what are your suggestions?"

"How about homemade chicken soup with dumplings? If you do the chicken and soup part, I'll do the vegetables and dumplings. But we have to have that on a night when I'm home from school early. Then how about that casserole with the macaroni and green peppers, carrots, dill, and hot dogs? That's easy and even if I get home later, it's fast. How soon do you have to have my other meals?

"And Josh, Ann wouldn't have you. As *you* say, 'Just kidding.' You didn't get this pot clean."

"Where'd I miss?"

We've got the monthly meal planning down to a fine art. In fact, since we purchased the computer, it's been even easier. Rachel and Josh put the menus we've planned over the past couple of years into a program (sometimes it's good to be a "saver") and made a grocery list for each meal. All we have to do is "cut and paste" and print the menus out for the month. Each week, we print out the grocery list. While we do have to change things occasionally, the major part of the planning is done—which saves us all time.

Phil doesn't balance the checkbooks anymore—just checks things over after Josh does the major work. Wonderful arrangement; Josh likes the challenge, and Phil has time for something else. Interesting how that arrangement happened ...

"You know, I really like our project business class."

"What's project business?"

"Didn't you have project business in eighth grade, Rachel?"

"No."

"Project business is where this dude came in from some school once a week."

"Josh, Mr. Grundman teaches business classes at the community college."

"Right, Mom. Anyway, this dude comes in, and he had us apply for a job. I applied for president of one of the companies he set up. We had to get references for our resumes, so I asked a couple of teachers who I've helped after school to write letters. Well, actually I wrote the letters during computer class and had them sign them—no extra work for the teachers that way."

"You did it during class?"

"Rachel, we were *supposed* to practice word processing, and it *was* my teacher's idea. You know how Dad always says teachers don't need extra work. Well, my computer teacher suggested I write the letters and have the teachers sign them. He was one of the teachers I've helped."

"I was chosen as president of one of the companies. It's been really neat. I got to hire people to work for me. Then we decided what kind of business we wanted."

"How'd you do that?"

"Well, Dad, this Grundman guy had several businesses to choose from. We did marketing. We wrote a letter, made copies, addressed envelopes, sealed them, and delivered them to Mr. Grundman. We received so much for each letter. He gave me a checkbook, so I put what we made in the checkbook. I wrote a check to pay everybody and one to him for the material to write the letters and envelopes and all that.

"Then he showed us how to balance a checkbook. Dad, I could balance our checkbooks now."

"Sure, Josh."

"No, really. Rachel has her own checking account since she started working, and she balances it. Why can't I balance yours?"

"Phil, why not let him try? It sure would save you some time. I'd be willing to let him balance mine. I hate doing it, and it's always such a hassle getting it to come out even."

"Well, if he can balance yours for the next couple of months, I'll let him balance the others."

"Gee, thanks, Dad! When do I start? Do I get a raise in my allowance for doing this?"

"Josh, if you get your mother's checkbook to balance, I'll take you to the Baseball Card Shoppe and get you that Ryne Sandberg card you've had your eye on."

I don't know how Josh does it, but since he's taken over balancing the checkbooks, even mine balances without too much trouble. Of course, I do try to be more conscientious about entering every check more accurately. Maybe it's helped him see how we use our salaries too. In fact, I like that Phil and Josh write out some of the standard checks, especially the ones to church and to pay tuition. That shows Josh where our priorities are.

There we are, back to time again. If I wouldn't have to drive to work, I could use that time to read or study my Sunday school lessons or even just sit back and relax. We sure could use a public transportation system. Oh, I get so aggravated driving sometimes! Like the other night when I was coming home. In fact, the whole day started off wrong as far as having enough time was concerned. There I sat in the car stewing. It was after five o'clock. There was so much traffic that the interstate was like a parking lot. There must have been an accident. Do I have enough gas to just sit here? Look at that driver passing everyone on the shoulder! Who does he think he is? I don't do well when I'm in a hurry. And I get so irritated with inconsiderate drivers.

What a day! It's hard getting everyone where they need to be and be where I have to be also. I feel like I've passed myself coming and going all day! This morning was a disaster!

"Mom, I need a ride to school this morning. Lisa just called and said her car won't start. Do you think we could pick her up? I told her we could."

"All right, Rachel. That means we'll have to step on it, though. How soon can you be ready to leave?"

"I still have to put in my contacts and brush my teeth. And I didn't make my lunch last night."

I wanted to panic. How was I going to finish getting dressed, probably help Rachel get her lunch together, pick up Lisa, fight traffic, and make it to the office in time for an early meeting?

"Mom, I can't find my gym shorts."

"Did you look in your drawer, Josh?"

"They're not in the drawer."

"Try your gym bag."

"I looked in the bag already."

"Did you leave them at school?"

"No. I don't know. I thought I brought them home. I've got to have my shorts or I can't take gym."

"Josh, I don't have time to help you look for your shorts right now. I've got to get Rachel to school, pick up Lisa, and I haven't put on my face yet!"

"You look pretty funny without a face. Just kidding. But I've got to have those gym shorts. Rachel, did you take my gym shorts?"

"Ruth, I'll make the bed and help Josh find his shorts. And you look great with the face you have. And I'm not kidding."

"Mom, I'll buy my lunch today. Can I wear your gold chain and earrings? You've spilled tea on your blouse. I'll start the car while you change your blouse."

It wasn't a perfect morning. I couldn't find a parking spot. I was minutes late for my meeting. And I missed the few minutes I have before work when I read my Bible. My day just doesn't seem complete without that.

I remember hearing or reading that Martin Luther would get up an hour earlier to add time for prayer to his day when he had more to do than he thought he could handle. It seems rather foolish to add something to your schedule when it is already overwhelmingly full. And sometimes I'm so tired. I can't imagine getting up an hour earlier. But I do appreciate the few minutes before I begin my work that I have with God—those quiet moments at my desk when I can read His Word and talk with Him before the phones start ringing, people demand my attention, the compute goes down, and little domestic crises occur.

"Good morning. Real Estate. Ruth speaking."

"Mom?"

"Josh?"

"Mom, I forgot my gym shorts at home."

"Josh, I thought Dad found them in your laundry basket."

"Yes, but I forgot to put them in my gym bag. Could you get them on your lunch hour and bring them to the school office? If I don't have my gym shorts, I can't take gym."

Well, there went my lunch hour. I was going to run some errands because the evening schedule was so hectic. But Josh is seldom so irresponsible. But he had a lot on his mind too. He had two tests that day. His team had a big soccer tournament during the week—that meant extra practice after school. More late, fast dinners!

As I sat in traffic, I remembered I forgot that I had to pick up some lunch things before going home. I sat there struggling with whether I should go to the store first, if I ever got out of the traffic, or just go home to make dinner. As it was, Phil, Rachel, and Josh had dinner well under way when I finally arrived home. It was a welcome sight.

We ended the day with Phil taking Rachel to the library and Josh to soccer practice at school since he was meeting with someone at school anyway. I did the pots and pans and headed for the store, then on to pick up Josh after his practice. And poor Phil came all the way home after his meeting only to realize he'd forgotten to pick up Rachel at the library. A bright spot during the day is the chats I have with the children driving them back and forth to wherever they have to be. Talk about quality time!

"Thanks for picking me up, Mom. Jeff sprained his ankle so his dad picked him up earlier. I didn't want to miss any of the practice or I could have gone with them."

"I'm glad to do it, Josh. Do you think Jeff's ankle is broken?"

"No. But the coach said to stay off of it and he'd look at it tomorrow. I'll call Jeff when I get home to see how it feels. He's a good player. Hope he can play in Saturday's game."

"Are you going to play too?"

"Sure. Probably won't start, but I'll play some. You know, Mom, I like soccer. I really like to play it. And I'm pretty good. I'll probably be good enough to make the team when I get to high school. But I'm not the best player. I could spend a lot of time sitting on the bench. But a team needs bench players. The first-string guys get tired and need relief."

"You don't mind not playing first string?"

"I mind. But I'm not *that* good. Actually, Mom, I like the coaching part. I'd like to be the one to say what plays to use, what strategy to try against another team."

"After Saturday's game, could we go to the mall? I need some new soccer shoes. These are too tight."

There are times when being the chauffeur is the best job a mom can have!

Quality time! Sometimes there seems to be no time to spend with my children and that concerns me. I want to be available if and when they need me. While I was at home with them when they were little, I was accessible. If something came up, I was there. What if they need me now? The bank frowns on personal phone calls. When they were both attending the school where Phil teaches, I always had it in the back of my mind they could go to their father. But that wasn't really always the way it was.

Just last spring, I risked my job because Josh was ill. He had been on a retreat from Friday night to Sunday afternoon, so when he came home tired and all he wanted to do was sleep, I let him stay home from school and sleep. By Wednesday morning, he was still tired and had developed a headache. Frowns from the bank or not, a quick call to the doctor had us taking him to the emergency ward. Tests showed he had some kind of viral infection. We started him on medication. Phil went on to school. I decided to stay home with Josh. The bank called asking when I'd be coming in; there were deadlines that had to be met.

I could hear the irritation in my employer's voice. I couldn't afford to lose my job. As old as Josh was, I didn't want to leave him alone. It was bad enough I'd done that for two days already. I remember praying and thinking about the conversations Phil and I had had about how God gave us these children as special gifts. God put them in our home for us to care for. They are special not only because we love them, but because they are God's special children. Caring for them is a trust from God. And the words of promise, "I will provide," still applied. Look at my namesake in the Bible. Ruth gave up her whole way of life to care for her mother-in-law. I'd rather give up my job than leave the son God gave into our care.

It isn't only emergencies when I'm concerned about being available to my family. When we're all going our separate ways, I sometimes feel out of touch with what is happening in their lives. Sometimes mealtime talk is "What's the schedule" conversation. And by bedtime, sometimes we're all so tired all we want to do is go to bed. I am reassured now and then that even if we don't have "our little chats," things are all right in our relationships. Rachel has become interested in so many new endeavors since starting high school. Seems like she's involved in some very worthwhile groups, like her Explorer troupe where she's with other young people interested in accounting as a profession. Last spring it seemed she was always going to their meetings.

"I'm home, Mom!"

"Hi, Rachel. How was your meeting?"

"It was fun. We nominated people for our new officers. My name is on for treasurer. I don't think I'll get it. Probably one of the older students will be elected."

"Do you want to be treasurer?"

"Maybe."

"It seems like such a long time since we've had a chance to just talk. I'm really sorry things are so rushed for me right now. Maybe we should plan a time to go out to dinner and shopping—well, maybe window shopping. Or I could drive you to school some mornings. The car seems to be a good place to talk."

"Mom, don't worry about spending time with me. I'm busy right now too. I don't even have time to think this week. Besides, Mom, we know we love each other. And I know you care abut me. If there's something I need to tell you, I'll let you know. Can we shop when things settle down a little? Maybe over our vacation? I need to get to my homework."

"Well, we'll have to schedule a night out—just the two of us. Maybe we can catch a few minutes together as we make dinner some evening or maybe Sunday."

Seems like Rachel's always liked the kitchen. I remember once when I was preparing dinner and she was sharing her homework with me. She didn't think I was paying attention to her because I kept on fixing food as she talked to me. Finally she came up to me, put her hands on each side of my face and said: "Mommy, I want to tell you about this. I can't see your eyes. Please listen." Undivided attention. How often do they want my undivided attention and

I keep on with what I'm doing?

And dear Phil. Does he feel neglected? We've never really talked about neglect. Sometimes when he's doing school work, I'll do some reading nearby. We have talked about the day when the children will need us less and we will have more time for one another. It's not as if we are out of touch, but it's not like the days when we were dating or first married. For now, I guess it's enough to know we are a family—a growing, changing family.

Change. That brings new situations, more decisions. My cousin Betty and her husband, Neal, have his mother to consider. As Betty said, "When our youngest left for college, I thought Neal and I would have some time for ourselves. I looked forward to the day when we could go out to dinner on the spur of the moment, when we'd have some privacy or not have to think about someone else's laundry. Well, we went from caring for our children to caring for a mother. In many ways, the situation is the same. But treating your parent as a child takes some real getting used to. Neal's mother is very dear but needs so much care. We just can't leave her alone. Sometimes it was hard to find baby-sitters. But grandma-sitters are nonexistent. Will we have to find a nursing home for her eventually? Will she be comfortable?"

What would we do if we had to care for one of our parents? Would I stay home? Maybe find a position with a company that provides elder care? Is there such a thing? How would we manage? My namesake took in her mother-in-law. God provided very richly for them. Look how Naomi enjoyed her family and her family enjoyed her. Perhaps the four of us should start thinking about this possibility. Our Sunday evening family night would be a good time to bring this up.

Time alone. I do enjoy some time alone. Thinking time. Time to talk to God. Time to work things out in my mind. Time to place my cares and concerns with God. Am I avoiding my responsibilities by asking God to handle problems and concerns in my life? How can I keep up with all that's going on in my world? God did promise to provide. I don't have all the answers. I don't know if I even ask all the right questions. But it has to be right to bring my concerns, and especially my thanks, to the God who has always shown me He loves me.

He loves me. When everything else seems upset and too much to cope with, I have His love. I see it best though Phil, Rachel, and Josh. Phil said home should be an oasis, a place to come for refreshment and quiet. I think God has given us that. But I think it's because He dwells in our house.

God. Family. Home. A place to go for refreshment. Do I hear Phil in the kitchen? Maybe he'll get a cup of coffee and join me out here. The air seems to be warmer.

> There is a time for everything, and a season for every activity under heaven:
> a time to be born and a time to die,
> a time to get up in the morning and a time to go to bed at night,
> a time to plan meals and a time to have dinner with your family,
> a time to do laundry and a time to teach the children how to do the laundry,
> a time to weep and a time to laugh,
> a time to go shopping and a time to pay bills,
> a time to drive to work and a time to be chauffeur,
> a time to teach Sunday school and a time to listen to a sermon,
> a time to clean house and a time to party,
> a time to listen and a time to speak,
> a time to love and a time to be loved,
> a time for running around and a time for peace.
> There is a time for everything, and a season for every activity under heaven.

An Encouraging Word

Ruth is a real-life person with whom many readers could identify. She has not experienced great tragedy or upheaval in her life. She is not going through a divorce or other great trauma. She does not have handicapped children or a delinquent teenager. Ruth is an ordinary working mother trying to juggle the demands of her husband, her children, her work, her church, and her emotional self.

Ruth appears to do it all, the perfect balancing act of the working mother. She walks the tight rope of being supermom without faltering. Although she longs for a quieter time, she seems to take pride in her success. So far all has gone well, just as Phil and she planned. It all seems so simple. Phil and she talk. They pray about it. They set a goal. They worry a little or a lot. They pray some more. They work hard. They succeed.

The Puritan work ethic seems to work well for Ruth. She is a woman who knows where she has been and where she is going. Her life is logical, purposefully planned, and sequential. Ruth is well-organized, efficient, and productive. She is the type of woman who could be trusted with a task.

Ruth has many practical ideas to share with other women who are struggling with time-management issues. She takes the words of Solomon in Ecclesiastes to heart. In her mind, there is a time for everything under the sun.

Ruth operates on a schedule. She prioritizes. She sticks to the task at hand. Ruth functions efficiently in the here and now. Ruth makes lists and schedules. She buys what is on her lists. She cooks the dishes listed on her menus. She keeps her commitments and sticks to her schedule. Ruth even schedules time for God, devotions, and Bible reading. Changes and unexpected small crisis are not what this lady thrives on. She is a person who much prefers a fast-paced planned program she can follow.

There is one thing that seems to break Ruth's pace. Caring for her children has a higher priority than her predesigned activities. Children come first. Ruth sees her children as gifts from God and as a trust. Her dedication to her children is admirable. Her anxiety over being a good mother, especially with Josh, borders on rescuing and the dreaded word of the '90s: codependency. It is hard to determine when one steps over the line, when one does too much for the other. Josh forgets his gym shorts. Josh gets a virus. These events were serious enough to set aside Ruth's schedule. Ruth could have let Josh experience natural consequences for forgetting his gym shorts instead of letting her guilt for not being a stay-at-home mother make the decision for her. His life would not have been ruined. She stayed home from work with Josh when he had the virus. There was no discussion with her employer. She decided Josh needed her. Ruth merely informed her employer she would not be in. She was willing to put her job in jeopardy to take this unauthorized time. She stayed home and cared for Josh whether he needed it or not. Ruth's reaction to her son's illness might have been on target, or it could have been an exaggerated reaction, a symptom of her own need to be needed, her tendency to be codependent.

Ruth increases her efficiency by taking advantage of modern technology. Her whole family uses the computer to help keep themselves organized and efficient. How many other women actually take the time to put their menus for the week, month, or year on a computer along with coordinated grocery lists? This is very time and budget efficient. Shopping lists cut down on the purchase of unnecessary items as well as the number of trips to the supermarket per week.

Delegation of authority is a natural consequence of Ruth's desire to stick to her task, to accomplish her goal. Ruth's pride does not get in the way of getting the job done, reaching the goal. She does not have the need to do everything herself. Josh ends up balancing the checkbooks for his parents as a young teen. Perhaps he has a career as a certified public accountant ahead of him. He also puts the menus and the grocery lists on the computer. Rachel helps, too, starting the car when the morning is rushed and there just isn't time for everything, especially something that was not already in the schedule.

As we listen and read between the lines, we notice that panic, anxiety, and the fear of loss of control loom beneath the surface of her organized exterior.

Financial concerns seem to be the biggest and most consistent source of stress for Ruth. When the children were young, she worried about where the next loaf of bread and the next bottle of milk would come from. She worried about the monthly bills, the house payment, and replacing the car sometime in the future. As the years pass, the dreaded day set aside for paying bills and balancing the checkbook has not proven to be a day for rejoicing. It is hard to determine if Ruth and Phil have trouble living within their means or have desires that reach beyond their pocketbook. It could be that Ruth (and Phil) are the type of people who would always worry and fret about money and bills even if they were millionaires. One thing is certain, they join thousands of others who find financial worries and concerns their number one stressor.

Ruth worries and is anxious about many things. She worries about whether she should go to work. She worries about how she can be the perfect wife and mother and still work. She worries about not spending enough time with her daughter. She worries about neglecting Phil. She worries about getting places on time. She worries about not being able to keep up the pace. She worries about losing control and somehow being left on the sidelines as life races by.

However, Ruth's anxiety is useful to her. She seems to have just enough anxiety to motivate her to stick to her goals and follow her schedule. She has developed this rigid time-management system as a way to manage her anxiety and the fast pace of her present stage of life. The secret is that it works.

Many of Ruth's time-management techniques are applicable to other women in other settings. Ruth's guidelines for a stress-controlled life are simple:
1. Set goals.
2. Schedule your day, hour by hour, minute by minute.
3. Stick to your schedule.
4. Make lists.
5. Use the lists.
6. Delegate authority.
   a. Assign specific tasks to others.
   b. Let them do their job without interference.
7. Prioritize.
8. Do one thing at a time.
9. Put some things aside for another day.

People who are as organized as Ruth sometimes pay a heavy price for their super scheduling. Working mothers can at times begin to feel bogged down. The humdrum of everyday life, the cooking, the cleaning, and the transporting of children all take their toll. The casual observer may only see the surface, the supermom, the successful working mother who appears to be handling it all. But life can become a habit and the person a machine.

Something happens to certain women caught in the same routine, the same rut, year after year. The working mother can become a robot who does her duties but her integrated personality no longer exists. Her personal thoughts and feelings, her needs as opposed to her children's needs, seem lost in the shuffle. She may feel her career is insignificant in status and take-home pay when compared with her husband's. It is easy for such a woman to slip into problems of low self-esteem, serious repression of her own feelings, focusing on the needs of others rather than being in touch with her own inner self. It's sometimes hard for the working mother to get attention for just being herself, doing ordinary things, and having ordinary feelings, wants, and desires. Somehow she may not feel she counts or is as important as other members in the family. Most women are trained to be sensitive and aware of the feelings and desires of others. Schedules are planned so everyone in the family has free time except the mother. Ruth surmises that her daughter will soon quit her job to have more time available for socialization, but is Ruth also planning a schedule change to include socialization and relaxation for herself?

Some women like Ruth become so driven by their tight schedules and their desire to be all things to their family and fellow employees that they begin to suffer emotional and physical symptoms. Migraine headaches, hiatal hernias, insomnia, or some form of an eating disorder might be warning signs that a more serious problem has developed. Depression, crying spells, or impulsively dumping anger on someone serve as warning signals that the emotions have been held in too long and are begging for expression. A few women even turn to addictive prescription pills or alcohol as a crutch doomed to fail. For some, the mild discomfort with life reaches a point where it becomes unbearable. Ruth copes but continues to ask herself if there might be another way.

Ruth effectively represses her own emotions. She controls her own anxiety but also appears to repress and control the part of her that enjoys the moment, is in touch with her feelings, and responds with enthusiasm to nature. We see a glimpse of her inner self, her communion with nature, in the beginning of her story. She is enjoying the quiet moment, the dogwood, the deck, a cup of coffee. One suspects there is another side to Ruth, one she has temporarily chosen to set aside in order to work and raise her family in the best and most efficient way she knows. One would even suspect there is a nostalgic part of her that sometimes wishes she were born in her grandmother's era, pre-World War II times, when the wife-mother working outside the home was a very unusual occurrence.

Ruth does not talk a lot about her own feelings but is quite sensitive to the feelings of others. She refers to Laura's pleasure in caring for her newborn infant and her pain at leaving the baby with a sitter. It is as if Laura's pleasure and pain are Ruth's. Ruth picks up on Phil's frustration about not earning enough money to support the family with his paycheck alone. She is sensitive to the children's enjoyment of life and is able to join them in a scheduled family slumber party. Ruth seems to be a self-sacrificing person who is almost unaware that she could assertively ask or do something for herself just for the fun of it. Even at work, Ruth describes herself as a good Samaritan, helping others when she can. She is a devoted mother, faithful wife, and a loyal employee. However, her style of living through the feelings of others sets her up to function in a codependent, unfulfilled manner.

Other Women

All females do not come out of the same mold. Each woman and mother is influenced from birth by her own genetic predisposition and the treatment she received from her parents as a child. Jobs, husbands, and children also leave their mark on the modern woman. Sometimes the children's personalities are so strong that mothers jokingly say that their child is raising them.

Trying to use Ruth's life as a model could give some successful working mothers great difficulty. Many women thrive on spontaneity, change, or the excitement of the moment. Such women rebel against what they would consider too much routine. They need to find something to help keep them from becoming too bored. Such women may never use a grocery list or even plan a menu except for special occasions and large groups. They may prefer to keep their options open and have many supplies on hand so that they can decide what to cook at the last minute.

Many women need to put a little creativity into every day. They prioritize, but at the last minute, they sometimes do several things at one time and jump from one project to another and then back. They hate setting goals, except for major ones, because it spoils their fun, the serendipity of their day.

These women would come up with a whole different list of ways for the working mother to manage stress.

1. Smell the roses.
2. Talk and laugh with your husband a lot.
3. Play with the children while they are still young.
4. Walk with a friend at lunch time.
5. Cry if you feel like it.
6. Throw a pebble in the pond and watch the ripples.
7. Feed the ducks.
8. Have enough food on hand so everyone can fix their own meals.
9. Call your mother on the phone and just chat.
10. Eat when you are hungry.
11. On the way to work, listen to music, enjoy the change of the seasons, the colors of fall, spring, and winter.
12. Take the children to the beach on your day off. Enjoy the sand squeezing through your toes.
13. Pay the bills before they are due.
14. Change the sheets when they are dirty.
15. Light a candle.
16. Plant a flower now and then.
17. Sleep when you are tired.
18. Enjoy and treasure each moment. Smile back at the moon.
19. Thank God for your children and ask for His guidance when they are having problems.
20. Hug someone several times a day.
21. Talk to God each day whenever you feel a need. Ask for His forgiveness and love.
22. Live in the freedom of the Gospel.

In all probability, all the items on the second list would not provide an effective style for Ruth. Most of the items on the list would not prove to be a good personality fit unless Ruth is able to slow down the treadmill of life. Maybe a time will come when she no longer wants to feel like a chicken with its head cut off. As time passes, Ruth may want to expand her responses to life's circumstances by moving at a reduced pace or by trying something new. Perhaps Ruth will want to develop a different sense of self, a new facet of her identity. Maybe she will want to add awareness of her feelings and interactions with her environment on a more regular basis. Maybe a time will come when Ruth will want to loosen up a bit. Maybe she will discover a new and deeper sense of control as she discovers there are some parts of her schedule she can let go. Maybe there is even more she can turn over to God. Perhaps some of the feelings of anxiety, panic, and loss of control will dissipate.

Working women need to find an integrated life-style. They need to try suggestions and ideas that have been effective in reducing stress. They need to mix and match ideas until the fit is comfortable. When the fit is too tight or too loose, they need to make adjustments. If they can't figure out what to change, they need to read a book, talk to a friend or a therapist or their pastor. They need to ask the Lord for His guidance in knowing whether it's time to laugh or cry, to work or play, to be scheduled or free, to love or be loved. They need to ask for God's forgiveness for the mistakes they make.

Like Ruth, women can take heart. Life is not static. Adjustment to change can be made. God's schedule and our schedule may not always match. Our times are in God's hands. Along with His grace and love, God promises: "There is a time for everything, and a season for every activity under heaven" (Eccl. 3:1 NIV).

Shirley Schaper

Reflection

- Do you see yourself operating like Ruth, using schedules, lists, and routines, or are you more "laid back"? What have you learned about your own work style that helps you succeed in working outside the home while raising a family? What have you learned from other working women that has helped you?
- Do you see a need for more or less organization in your life? Do you ever feel like a slave to clock and calendar?
- What value do you see in setting goals and priorities? How hard is it for you to stick to your "game plan"?
- When you feel pressured, how do you treat your family? your co-workers? yourself?
- Make a list of everything *you* need to be a whole person. Circle those things on your list you already have. What is left? Why are those things missing in your life?
- Who are you? What roles do you play? Is your personal identity defined solely by those roles? Why or why not? What or who has shaped you into the person you are today?
- Keep a list of all your activities for a few days. Make a list of things you would like to do but may not be doing. What changes will you need to make? How do your priorities show/give witness to your faith and trust in God? Read Luke 10:38–42 and Luke 12:22–31. Meditate on 1 Cor. 10:31 and 2 Cor. 4:16–18.
- Make your own list of suggestions and secrets for "success" that you might share with other working women struggling to balance home and career.

Lord of all time and talent and treasure,
Giver of all good gifts,
Father and Brother and Savior,
Patient Teacher and Powerful Spirit,
You are my life and my strength.

Centered in You,
I know who I am,
Beloved daughter,
Precious child,
Gifted woman,
Lover, and friend.

As steward of Your gifts,
I want to spend wisely.
Help, Lord.
It isn't easy.

Make me wise.
Help me find the treasure
in Your Word,
the treasure in the people You have given me
in my life.

Help me find the time
for what You tell me is important.
Help me find the talents
You have on deposit within me.

And then I will rejoice
in Your guidance,
Your forgiveness,
Your acceptance
of me.

Amen.